In life, as in business, our ability to develop and grow defines who we are and what we become. Fit to Grow *provides practical insight and sound advice on how to transform a business. The book offers a prudent and viable path towards growth and success.*

EDWARD JOHNSON
PRESIDENT & CEO | BETTER BUSINESS BUREAU

Mark Richardson has the ability to explain complex ideas simply. His book is not "consultant-speak" but real life solutions, tried and tested in his own successful business. Now is a good time for all of us to reinvent our companies and ourselves. Read Mark's book to help you do so.

PETER H MILLER HON AIA
PRESIDENT | RESTORE MEDIA

Fit to Grow *is a must read for any business owner who wants to excel and grow in today's challenging marketplace. Authored by a Hall of Famer in the Remodeling Industry with years of experience in leadership and "know how" that will certainly benefit all business leaders.*

MIKE BOZICH
VP | HENKEL

Mark Richardson knows what it's like to have business growth goals that at times seem unobtainable. Mark understands the keys to business growth that are relevant—whether your operation employs five or 5,000. I'm delighted for his business success. He has helped others follow in his footsteps, thanks to his key themes and poignant questions. Fit to Grow *is filled with inspiring ideas to help influence your business and accomplish your goals.*

DAVID LINGAFELTER
PRESIDENT | MOEN INCORPORATED

Mark Richardson's new book, Fit to Grow, *provides incredible insight for business owners who are in the process of analyzing and strategizing the growth of their business in this new, emerging economy. The economic collapse changed the industry dramatically. The path to building our businesses back requires new strategies and perspectives that Mark has keenly outlined in this book. The timing of it couldn't be better. Mark's unique insights are based on decades of hard earned, practical experience of "doing it successfully" himself combined with many years of successfully advising businesses, corporate advisory boards and related industry associations from the board level to operations. I highly recommend this book as the top read for 2013.*

KEVIN P. O'NEILL
GENERAL MANAGER & COO | WELLBORN CABINET, INC.

The wisdom Mark so generously shares in Fit to Grow, *once again, provides a road map to ensure any business is poised to achieve growth. The conversation about the "pace" of a business is one we have regularly. Is it a sprint or a marathon? Mark has taught me the value of steady, sensible growth and how to achieve it. Always a pioneer, even in these changing times, Mark helps us make sense out of things. He's a master.*

LISA BIEN-SINZ
SENIOR VICE PRESIDENT | INSIDE EDGE COMMERCIAL INTERIOR SERVICES, LLC

So many of us have been hunkered down in survival mode that growth seems like a distant memory. Thank you for the wakeup call to action: it's time to make things happen.

ANDY WELLS
CO-OWNER | NORMANDY REMODELING

Mark Richardson is a thought leader in the area of business growth. He has built companies and advised many others. His advice in Fit to Grow *is timely, practical and from the trenches. Mark is also a natural teacher and public speaker. Make sure this book is on your early in 2013 reading list!*

ANDREW J. SHERMAN
PARTNER | JONES DAY
AUTHOR OF *HARVESTING INTANGIBLE ASSETS* AND OF *ESSAYS ON GOVERNANCE*

As a student of our industry and those that have a clear vision of the future, I think this work is an invaluable reference for those with a commitment to grow. Mark writes in such a way as to engage the reader; he also challenges the reader to place a greater value on people within the organization. His assertion that the customer experience is the launching pad for continued success should be the mantra of all businesses.

CHRIS EDWARDS
CEO | THE TOTAL COMPANIES

As a business owner, I find Mark's insights on business to be an invaluable resource. His step-by-step approach to business growth moves far beyond the theoretical by addressing concepts that are easily actionable and highly relevant. His approach can be applied across any industry and has improved my outlook, approach and most importantly, my bottom line.

JAMES NESBITT
CO-FOUNDER | WALL-TO-WALL STUDIOS, INC.

Fit to Grow *is an education in mirroring great companies. Surround yourself with a great team. Know your numbers. The bottom line is to grow. Always do the right thing. Follow your passion.*

GARY MARROKAL
MARROKAL DESIGN AND REMODELING

Once again Mark has written a very timely and insightful book that everyone in business should read. In his book, he focuses on twelve key components that any business, regardless of industry, should analyze if they want to maximize growth. His work with countless organizations of all size and industry gives him keen insight into success today. I highly recommend this book to every businessperson looking to grow their company.

CHRIS C. EDELEN
PRESIDENT AND CEO | LEAF GUARD BY BELDON INC.

Mark Richardson is a reference not just in the remodeling world but also in small business development circles. Upon reading his last book How Fit Is Your Business?, *I decided to order the book for every VELUX sales rep so they can understand the business struggles of their customers better. I also ordered a book for many of our "5-Star" business partners so they could read up on how to improve their business health. In our industry, skylight installers and small remodelers are always excellent craftsmen but they do not always know all the basic tricks to keep a business healthy and profitable. Mark's books address those issues head on.*

STEPHAN MOYON
DIRECTOR OF SALES | VELUX AMERICA INC.

As usual, Mark Richardson's timing is impeccable. After four or five years of a very challenging market, those companies still in business or starting, can once again explore growth. Just as his last book was excellent for its time, this book looks at just the issues we need to be thoughtful about. In our industry there is no one better than Mark to give us the key insights that will build the foundation for profitable growth in the near and long term.

TOM KELLY
OWNER | NEIL KELLY INC.

By using the principles in Mark's first book, How Fit Is Your Business?, *we were able to increase our home sales for 2012 in the DC market by 20%. With the insight of his new book,* Fit to Grow, *we are planning to expand our success despite the economic transition and challenges of 2013.*

GEORGE W. LODGE
FEDERATED REAL ESTATE GROUP

Many small businesses grow to fit the vision and talents of their founder. In his new book, Mark Richardson breaks this paradigm and challenges business leaders whether they are Fit to Grow. *Mark adeptly questions traditionally held business practices and their compatibility with the realities of today's marketplace. With insights grounded in his many years of experience and involvement in numerous aspects of the home improvement industry, business leaders are well advised to follow this practical guide that will certainly help get their businesses in shape for success in the years ahead.*

JEFF SHAWD
VICE PRESIDENT, MARKETING | GE CAPITAL

In business, as in life, when we begin with a few basic tenets by which to measure our decisions, difficult questions come more easily into focus. By determining to make the themes from Mark's Fit to Grow *a priority, we are able to greatly reduce the stress that results from certain situations. If "People Are My Greatest Asset," my attitude toward people will reach a higher level and dictate my outward actions. When I "Define Success" I am able to center my thoughts and performance rather than to chase some intangible, albeit lofty, cloud called success. These themes along with the ten others in* Fit to Grow *can simplify and strengthen the way you conduct your business...and your life!*

JOY KILGORE
PRESIDENT | PRIME

FIT TO GROW

MARK G RICHARDSON

FIT TO GROW

12 BUSINESS THEMES FOR GROWTH

Advantage

Published by Advantage, Charleston, South Carolina.
Member of Advantage Media Group.

ADVANTAGE is a registered trademark and the Advantage colophon is a trademark of Advantage Media Group, Inc.

Printed in the United States of America.

ISBN: 978-159932-400-5
LCCN: 2013931096

This publication is designed to provide accurate and authoritative information in regard to the subject matter covered. It is sold with the understanding that the publisher is not engaged in rendering legal, accounting, or other professional services. If legal advice or other expert assistance is required, the services of a competent professional person should be sought.

Advantage Media Group is proud to be a part of the Tree Neutral® program. Tree Neutral offsets the number of trees consumed in the production and printing of this book by taking proactive steps such as planting trees in direct proportion to the number of trees used to print books. To learn more about Tree Neutral, please visit **www.treeneutral.com**. To learn more about Advantage's commitment to being a responsible steward of the environment, please visit **www.advantagefamily.com/green**

Advantage Media Group is a publisher of business, self-improvement, and professional development books and online learning. We help entrepreneurs, business leaders, and professionals share their Stories, Passion, and Knowledge to help others Learn & Grow. Do you have a manuscript or book idea that you would like us to consider for publishing? Please visit advantagefamily.com or call 1.866.775.1696.

ACKNOWLEDGMENTS

Acknowledgments are an author's indulgence. They are personal, often obscure, and have very little to do with the average reader, at least not directly.

However, as I have grown older and somewhat wiser, I have come to realize that our lives are made up of series of moments and passages, some purposeful, some accidental, and all stemming from our interaction with the people around us. Our natural inclination is to see order in chaos and impose design on randomness. Writing acknowledgments, I have now discovered, is as good a place to start that process as any. In fact, in the spirit of improving and growing yourself and your business (which is what this book is all about), writing your own acknowledgments is the perfect way to isolate the moments of truth that have shaped your life, bringing to mind all those who helped you along the way. In my case, there are many.

I begin with my parents, James and Sheila Richardson, who laid my life's foundation, which is both solid and broad. The environment they provided offered many choices with little risk of failure or injury.

I also want to acknowledge Tom Regan, my architecture advisor at Virginia Tech and my first real mentor. Professor Regan taught me how to think. He helped me understand that architecture was only the vehicle for my life's journey; he helped me see things through a wider lens and adopt a perspective that was less literal. He showed me that we are not so much a product of what we see but of how we see and taught me that if we look through the right lens, we will find much to see in every aspect of the world.

Next is Fred Case. Fred created a very fertile landscape upon which I have been able to flourish and grow. When I struggled to find the next challenge that would fuel my passion, Fred provided me with an environment in which I could conduct experiments and practice. Many of the ideas I share in this book spring directly from that nurturing ground and from our partnership.

In addition, I want to thank my wife, Margie: in the way she nurtures our three wonderful children—Jessica, Jamie, and Brett—the way she provides welcoming comforts in our home, and the way with which she effortlessly removes any and all natural obstacles to my growth, she adds color to a life that would otherwise be black and white. We have very different personalities, and without Margie, my life would be incomplete.

Many require thanks, however, Joy Kilgore and Sam Imhof have been true partners and sounding boards in my professional journey that have resulted in many new creations and opportunities for the future.

Many others have served as my life advisors and supporters: John Richardson, Laurie Griel, Kermit Baker, Patrick O'Toole, Mike Allen, Andrew Sherman, Peter Miller, Sal

Alfano, Chris Dana, Tony Mancini, Bill Millholland, Adam Witty, Mike Bozich, Mike Ethier, Bruce Case, Rick Matus, George Weissgerber, and Joaquin Erazo.

Thanks also to the many other family members, friends, and acquaintances who have supported me over the years and who may have offered me an insight or tidbit that I unconsciously adopted or incorporated into my thinking without being aware of the source.

—MARK G. RICHARDSON

FOREWORD

Business is a game; it's the greatest game alive.

—Tom Watson

In September 2003 I took over as editor of a magazine devoted to the business-information needs of remodelers. I came to the job with years of experience, first as a reporter, then as a business writer, and finally as a business writer serving a similar profession: new-home builders. Therefore, I felt quite confident in applying that experience and immediately pouring it into articles that remodelers would readily consume. I was so wrong. I can only describe the period that followed as one of culture shock. Whereas successful homebuilders often think like manufacturers—highly focused on systems and processes and somewhat removed from the day-to-day interaction with their clients—successful remodelers are cut from an entirely different cloth.

To get clients through the often-emotional process of remodeling their homes, remodelers must possess incredible people skills on top of the requisite construction and business knowledge. To the uninitiated, remodeling seems like a straightforward business. And it certainly can be. But the numerous variables associated with opening up walls, the stresses of working side-by-side with clients every day, the intricacies of properly pricing jobs can make remodeling an entrepreneur's nightmare. Mark Richardson, then president of Case Design Remodeling, was among a small handful of people during my early days covering the industry who took the time to walk me through the nuances of succeeding in the remodeling business, and more generally, what it takes to succeed as an entrepreneur.

An architect by training, Richardson came to the industry in the early '80s with a creative mind and applied it not only to the art of remodeling but also the business of remodeling. In his three decades of leadership at Case, the company grew and prospered phenomenally, and along the way he helped pioneer several new ways of doing business. He was an early and ardent proponent of the design-build process as a successful business model in remodeling. He was part of a team that established and grew one of the largest national, full-service, remodeling operations. For ten years he hosted a home-improvement radio show and in the process found his voice not only as a public speaker but also as a business columnist. For years he dispensed sage advice in a business where failure is frequently the rule rather than the exception to it.

Over the years many accolades have followed. He is a member of the NAHB Remodeling Hall of Fame. He won an Ernst and Young Entrepreneur of the Year award. He is a Fellow at Harvard University's Joint Center for Housing

Studies. Today, in addition to his work as a consultant and speaker, he writes the "Think Business" column for the magazines I help edit, *Professional Remodeler* and *Professional Builder*. In short, what makes Richardson a singular figure is not only his tenure among the top leaders in remodeling but also the creativity, clarity, and perspective with which he is able to communicate his leading business concepts.

Fit to Grow is the natural extension of Richardson's first book, *How Fit Is Your Business?* And I was pleased to be among the few who were able to read an early edition because, over the years, I have seen many of these ideas presented to groups of remodelers and entrepreneurs and have noted their enthusiastic, smiling, nodding reactions. So much about business today requires proper perspective. Through extremely apt metaphors backed by clear, concrete examples, Richardson's ideas consistently hit the mark in person and in print.

Coming now, in the wake of a prolonged recession, *Fit to Grow* is perfectly timed to help entrepreneurs evaluate their businesses as would athletes preparing for the big game. Surviving in business is one thing, but growing is another matter entirely. Ironically, far too many small business owners have grown complacent in their efforts to root out business weaknesses. This is the result of a hunkered-down, survival-mode mentality. At the same time, this book does not dictate or preach. Richardson's twelve, main "business themes to grow by" are offered à la carte. If you gravitate toward ideas relating to leadership or communication, latch on to them. And (perhaps most significantly) use them together and discover how one plus one often equals three. Richardson argues that the real opportunity for growth essentially resides in the synergies that are created when two or more of these proven themes are merged together. It is similar to what is happening in the world of physical fitness.

Around the country today, more Americans than ever are discovering the benefits of cross training. Led by an instructor, cross-training programs are group activities. Participants move through a series of exercises that alternate between various muscle groups in the body. Cross training is synergistic. And it results in a more balanced and well-rounded fitness regime. *Fit to Grow* is cross training for your business. Richardson makes a strong case that learning basic business themes, committing to them, and working on them together with your team can improve your business fitness. It is a balanced approach that will certainly make your company more able to take on more business.

—Patrick L. O'Toole

Editorial Director and Publisher
Professional Remodeler magazine

TABLE OF CONTENTS

Why Are Business Themes Important?

47

Twelve Business Themes for Growth

51

1. PEOPLE: **PEOPLE ARE YOUR GREATEST ASSET**
2. COMMITMENT: **INVEST TIME TO IMPROVE**
3. MASTERY: **IF YOU GIVE, YOU GET**
4. ACTION: **LISTEN, LEARN, AND THEN RESPOND**
5. EXPERIENCE: **BUSINESS IS ABOUT THE EXPERIENCE**
6. PLANNING: **IF YOU FAIL TO PLAN, THEN PLAN TO FAIL**
7. EXPECTATIONS: **EXCEED EXPECTATIONS**
8. COMMUNICATION: **IT IS OUR OBLIGATION TO COMMUNICATE, NOT THE RESPONSIBILITY OF OTHERS TO UNDERSTAND**
9. RELATIONSHIPS: **CREATE CLIENTS AND BUSINESS WILL FOLLOW**
10. SYNERGY: **ONE PLUS ONE EQUALS THREE**
11. PACE: **AGGRESSIVE BUT REALISTIC**
12. SUCCESS: **DEFINING SUCCESS**

INTRODUCTION

Conformity is the jailer of freedom and the enemy of growth.

—John F. Kennedy

Are you Fit to Grow? This is not a question many business owners ask themselves. They may ask one of the following questions instead: "How do I grow?" "How do I expand my market share?" "How do I increase the value of my business so I can exit it or retire?" Yet, while they may ask these questions, they do not spend much energy looking in the mirror and taking a good assessment of where they are or understanding some of the fundamentals required for growth.

The business growth dynamic can be rewarding but also risky. A greater percentage of businesses fail in their attempts to grow. The Small Business Administration (SBA) has noted that three out of five small businesses fail within the first five years; in some industries, such as home construction and remodeling, about nine out of ten fail within ten years. These numbers do not lie. Focusing on understanding the business growth is critical to a business's basic health and survival.

So, why do I use colorful language when asking if you, as a business owner, are "Fit to Grow"? In my earlier book, *How Fit Is Your Business?*, I drew a metaphorical parallel between business fitness and personal health and fitness. In that book I break down the fundamental misconceptions that can result in an unhealthy business and provide a basic understanding of business health. I take the reader through a ten-point business fitness checkup, similar to what you would receive if you went to the doctor for a physical. In the next part of the book, I focus, as a doctor would, on a prescription and plan for better business fitness or health.

In my previous book I focused on the fundamentals of business fitness and helped readers assess their current business's overall health. In that book, I did not address how to prepare for that business growth. Metaphorically, in business, just as in baseball, you need to know how to throw, hit, and catch before you can play and enjoy the game. Similarly, as in baseball, you need to understand much more, such as baseball strategies, team dynamics, and individual roles and expectations, all of which contribute to making a winning team.

A few natural or obvious questions are these: Why don't business owners know and understand business fitness and the ten criteria for a healthy business? Why don't business owners understand how to position their companies for growth? I believe the answers lie primarily in the motivation for and ease of getting into businesses in the first place, along with a lack of basic business education. Most business owners start a business because of a passion. This passion could be centered on a product, craft, or skill; it could be about seeking independence; it could be a belief that owning a business is equivalent to achieving the American dream; or it could be a means to greater wealth or security. Whatever the motivation, this passion far outweighs the desire to invest time and learn the basics about business acumen and growth.

Most owners of business start-ups spend little time developing a meaningful business plan or a detailed road map. They may have studied the competitive landscape to determine how a product would fit, but they have not studied the game of business. They devote very little time to understanding the phases of business growth and the knowledge and adjustments required along the way. Unlike a developing athlete, who works with a coach to develop skills and improve, most business owners opt to go it alone and learn from trial and error (at a very high cost, possibly failure). If this paragraph describes you, you are not alone. In fact, you are in the vast majority of business owners. So, what can you do from here?

While reading my first book is not a prerequisite to understanding this book, I would highly recommend doing so. *How Fit Is Your Business?* provides a baseline, introducing a language and business mindset that makes this book clearer. Through my first book, I enable you to conduct an assessment of your business fitness and determine whether you are ready to grow. In it I also provide tips on getting ready for growth so that you are more likely to succeed.

In the following chapters I will set the stage by discussing the importance of change. Without developing the conviction to change your mindset, it will be difficult for you to appreciate the insights I offer in this book. First, I will help you understand growth (the definition may not be as obvious as you think). Second, I will discuss developing the right culture, which is so critical for growth (this is like preparing to run a marathon: it takes time and patience). Lastly, I will share the twelve themes that you should adopt in your organization to achieve healthy growth. You may have a few of these themes in place presently, but they should all fit together, collectively, like puzzle pieces. With all of the puzzle pieces in place, you will have a solid foundation for successful and sustainable growth.

You may choose to read this book in its entirety and then go back and focus on specific themes or chapters later. You may also want to use the book as a guide for your team members so they can begin discussing the subject of growth. Alternatively, you may find the contents of this book validate much of what you are currently doing; through reading, you will have greater conviction to grow and be successful. However you decide to leverage the tools provided in my book, I encourage you to commit to understanding growth fully before diving in and beginning to grow your business.

Change. . .or Become Irrelevant

Change is the law of life. And those who look only to the past or present are certain to miss the future.

—John F. Kennedy

"Change is the law of life," as Kennedy observed. We all know what it means. We all change whether we like it or not. We change physically through our natural aging process. Our tolerance for risk changes with time and circumstances. We also have the ability to change through our decisions and actions. Some change is good, and some is not. As we understand and improve on most aspects of business and life, our perspectives and priorities may change too. Change is a given. It is just a way of life.

Making change a business mindset does not mean you should just acknowledge the obvious. It means you should start controlling the change process proactively. It means you should be forward thinking as you start investing in change and preparing for that change in a healthy manner. Adding the idea that you become irrelevant without change makes addressing that change essential.

I first heard the phrase, "If a business is not changing, it will become irrelevant," from a very successful friend, Chris Edelen, when we won an award for growing his business in a tough down-market. This remark struck a chord in me at many levels, and it has become an integral part of my growth mindset. While we can continue to reflect philosophically on the subject of change, I believe it may be more productive to focus on change more pragmatically.

I would like to begin with the second part of this quotation first, because it is where we get our conviction to make change a priority. When I first heard my friend use the word *irrelevant* in this context, I got a sick feeling in my stomach; the word conjured up an image of a graveyard of businesses into which people had put heart and soul. Why had these businesses become irrelevant? Their owners had focused too much on the here and now, not on changing to respond to future demands. They had not been listening to the marketplace or their clients. They had lost key talent to other companies who had offered those employees a future, not just a job. They and their companies had become irrelevant.

Becoming irrelevant is like receiving the kiss of death. Imagine being irrelevant as a spouse or a parent. What an awful thing to endure. Being irrelevant is the ultimate insult, both personally and professionally. An irrelevant athlete is cut or retires (and very few are positioned for another career). In business, being irrelevant may be the difference between staying open or not. First and foremost you should make maintaining company relevance part of your business operations, both as a priority and a way of thinking.

Change is a complex subject. While changing is a given, the why, what, when, and how questions should become part of your process and mastery. Most people (including, it is likely, many on your team) have a difficult time adjusting to and managing change (especially if they do not have total buy-in). The process of changing can be as important as the change itself. Some changes are natural and are part of basic evolution or updates. Some changes can be simple, like a golfer adjusting a golf grip, thereby improving his or her score by several strokes. Other changes can be more complex, like a new brand message, a new product, or a new service.

Joaquin Erazo, chief marketing officer of Case Design Remodeling, introduced me to a great phrase or question that I often use when I am counseling business leaders. I ask them, "Are you in the wave?" Those who have spent time at the beach watching the waves or body surfing know that being *in the wave* means hitting the wave at the right time, with the right position and posture. If you are ahead of the wave (which I have painfully been, many times, both in body surfing and in business), you might get hurt and spend a great deal of energy getting nowhere. If you are behind the wave, you will not be propelled ahead in the water or ahead of your competition. To be in the wave, you must adjust and go for it. To be in the wave in business, you must act at the right time, with the right knowledge, and with the right energy.

Change (or the act of being in the wave) can be the difference between success and failure in many aspects of business and life. If we accept change as an integral part of our thinking process, we have the basic foundation for growth. We can remove some of our blinders and look at growth through different lenses.

Defining Growth

You can't do today's job with yesterday's method
and still be in business tomorrow.

—Alfred Chandler

When I originally conceived this book, I thought I would use a different title: *Business Themes to Live By*. I shared an audio interview with a business colleague, who replied, "Thank you for sharing *Business Themes to Grow By* with me." Initially, I thought he was a little sloppy and had got the book title wrong, but I later realized he had given me the word describing the why behind this book.

Some say that if a business is not growing, it is dying. While this sounds a little harsh and is probably not completely true, the statement does force you to think about the subject of growth. The more you can define and comprehend growth, the more you will be prepared to grow.

At many companies, owners define business growth by top line sales, market share, team or asset increases, and profitability. Many other elements of growth are important to a business too. Think of key members on your team today and imagine where they will be three years from now. They need to grow both in their skills and in their contributions to the business. If they are not given the opportunity to grow (and they are very good) they will leave the company. The asset or team member will be lost, and the business will suffer. *USA Today* did a survey in 2010 that revealed about 30 percent of a business's team members would leave the businesses they worked for when the economy stabilized. I believe the primary reason employees leave a company is a lack of growth and opportunities.

Business growth can also appear via a number of other fronts, such as client satisfaction ratings, efficiencies, or new products or services. In your business, you may focus on growth related to removing uncertainty or on creating a more stable environment through diversification, product blend, or a new client base.

One of the most important areas of growth is in your leadership growth. Many years ago, I met a man who was in his early forties and had created a very successful technology business. I asked him about his next big goal or area of focus. He said, "Right now, I am looking for someone to fire me." As you can imagine, I was a little taken aback by this notion. However, after some reflection, I realized he was talking about his own growth. For leaders, growth also involves their own transitions and passages. One of the only ways a leader can grow is by developing others to take over his or her current role(s). In essence, that leader's replacement will then push him or her forward to a new opportunity that can be very fulfilling. Imagine it is five years from now and you are doing exactly what you are doing now. For most people, that sounds pretty scary and a little depressing.

As you contemplate the meaning of *growth* for yourself or your business, try this exercise. Write down five to ten ways you define growth at your business. To reinforce the point, ask some of your key team members to do the same. Once you have a consistent way of defining *growth* in your business, list all the benefits of growing. While this may seem like an academic exercise, it will do several things. First, it will create a dialogue on a subject often infrequently discussed. Second, it will show how well aligned you are with others whom you trust and respect. Third, it will give you the conviction to make both growing and the knowledge of how to grow a priority.

The Business Dynamic

It is not the strongest of the species that survive, nor the most intelligent, but the most responsive to change.

—Charles Darwin

Business is dynamic, not static. The economy goes up and down. The relationship between a business and customers varies over time. Client expectations and priorities change. How we communicate with our clients, our team members, and our alliances evolves and adjusts based on the technologies at our fingertips and on the environment.

You have probably heard many adages or quotations about the dynamic nature of things: "Life is a journey, not a destination." "The future isn't what it used to be." "The only constant is change itself." We know these statements are true. Unfortunately, many business owners treat processes and formulas for success like recipes for baking cookies or prescriptions for sinus infections. This may be because many people are wired to check answers off their to-do lists and move on to the next challenge or problem to solve. This mindset could also be a fundamental philosophical disconnect from, or misunderstanding of, how dynamic a business really is. Managing this dynamic can be very frustrating, especially if you are not looking though the right pair of lenses.

Many years ago I began thinking about this subject with regard to our home remodeling business. At the time, my company was a relatively small, local business, its success less dependent on processes and systems and more dependent on individual talent, sweat, personal beliefs, and passions. Because of local success and some timely national media attention, builders and remodelers around the country started contacting the company, asking if my team members could help them improve and grow their businesses. What started as monthly inquiries became daily occurrences, and so, due to entrepreneurial spirit, we decided to launch a national remodeling franchise business.

Deciding to take something that you do naturally every day and attempting to teach it to others can be a very interesting yet frustrating process. How do you communicate and train others to understand insights gained through hundreds of years of collective experience? In our company's case, our first step was simply to write down what we were doing at the organization, along with why and how we were doing it. This process can be overwhelming, even at the big-picture level, but it becomes particularly thorny as you drill down into the many small details. However, the process of articulating concepts and processes that have been taken for granted at your organization can also reveal whether or not you are aligned with other team members.

As we analyzed each process, rule by rule and solution by solution, my team members and I realized we had more variables than constants. In many cases, we produced many answers to the same question. For example, some team members proposed sending a remodeling client a list of expectations during construction, while others proposed sitting down with a client over a cup of coffee and walking him or her through the process. Both methods are good ones. Home remodeling can be a scary process, and sometimes showing a little patience is better. While there were, obviously, many black-and-white solutions to the problems we encountered, much of what we did and many of our team members' successful approaches fell into a gray area. Working together, we learned that the real mastery in our business lay in our team members' appreciation for, and ability to work within, many shades of gray. Communicating about those gray areas is the true subject of this book.

The revelation that the guidelines for our business could not be simply written down as a specific prescription or outlined in a rule book led my team and me to develop our *Themes to Live By*. First articulated more than fifteen years ago, these themes became a guiding light for us in the aftermath of the 9/11 terrorist attacks. They have remained relevant, both in the boom times of 2003 through 2005 and in the crash of 2008. These themes required a change in perspective and were essential to the company's significant growth.

To understand change, growth, and the dynamic nature of business, you must look at these topics through the correct filter for your business. Through this filter, or lens, you will begin to see and understand the real concept of business culture.

Business Culture

A culture of discipline is not a principle of business; it is a principle of greatness.

—Jim Collins

For many business leaders and their employees, especially the newest team members, the connotation of *business culture* is equivalent to Jim Jones, the cult leader, passing out Kool-Aid for everyone to drink. Most know what the outcome was in that situation. While I suppose someone could argue there is some truth to this image as it relates to corporatespeak, I wish to stress that there is a deeper, more practical importance to understanding the subject of business culture. Just as we use them to process many lessons in business and in life, we seek metaphors we can use to see this subject through the right lens.

The one metaphor that has made some light bulbs go off on this subject, so to speak, comes from the sports world. In business culture training sessions, I typically ask a group of new team members (mostly Americans) whether they like the sport of professional football. Predictably, from a group of twenty people, at least fifteen will say yes. Some group members are big fans of football; others may have a more casual interest, yet they still enjoy watching a good game on a Sunday afternoon. The next question I ask the group is why they like football. I ask why they take their valuable time and invest it in watching this specific sport or entertainment. They consistently say they enjoy "the action and hitting of the game," "the teamwork that is displayed," "the relation to the game's history or tradition," "the memories of playing as kids," and "the amazing level of talent and skill displayed."

Next, I ask whether the group members know how many points a touchdown is worth or what gesture the umpire uses to communicate when a team scores a touchdown. Again, as you would predict, all of the fifteen fans (and maybe a few others) know the answers to these questions. Then, I ask a deeper question about the yardage for offsides or pass-interference penalties. As you would imagine, only the more serious football fans know the answers. I then throw them a curveball question, asking how many people in the group can't wait to go home and watch a professional rugby match on television. The group members look at me as if I am speaking a foreign language. They are puzzled as to why I would even think of such a ridiculous question, and rarely do any of them raise a hand. I then ask whether professional rugby matches have hard-hitting action, a strong element of teamwork, a rich tradition or history, and a high level of playing. I ask how points are scored in rugby, and rarely does anyone know. I ask about some basic terms, such as a *scrum* or a *ruck*. Again, these words usually elicit chuckles, since they sound like a foreign language.

The power of this rugby-versus-football metaphor is that the audience begins to understand what *culture* is all about and, most significantly, why culture is important. A sport is not meaningful or enjoyable unless the audience understands the game's goals, rules, some history (or the why behind the sport), potential for success, and who is doing what on the field.

This concept of understanding a game or culture is equally important in business. Once you set aside the connotations of "drinking the Kool-Aid" or corporatespeak, you can begin to build a strong foundation for a business culture. Without understanding this platform, the team members who make up a business will have a difficult time being in sync and growing the organization. The twelve themes I will outline in this book are critical to creating the right business culture. These business themes are like glue; they hold the parts of the business together. They give the business representatives tools to use so they know when to turn right or left, or when to slow down or speed up. These business themes are not, however, the game's history, specific processes, and rules; rather, they are the framework team members can use to put these concepts in place. Without the themes, it is difficult for a business to have momentum or inertia. Without the themes, a business may have talents, but those talents are not working in unison. A business's members must have a commitment and focus to the organization's sticks and bricks; they must also know *how* to think about business. With these ingredients, they will have a formula for growth that can lead to success.

Why Are Business Themes Important?

Drive thy business; let not that drive thee.

—Benjamin Franklin

Imagine a world without rules. There would be complete chaos. The world could not function. It is a crazy idea. Rules come in different forms and at many different levels. Some rules, such as speed limits, are very specific. Other rules that are broader, such as "Love thy neighbor as thyself," allow individuals to interpret each rule through their own personal filters. There are other rules that make the enjoyment and experience of an activity more fulfilling, such as guidelines in sports. Rules allow us to understand what we need to master and take our own game to a different level. While rules can be restrictive, they can also make a game more understandable and enjoyable.

As we reflect on almost all aspects of our lives, we realize that we function effectively because of the rules and themes by which we live. These themes allow our society to function smoothly. These themes or beliefs differentiate us from each other and help to define us.

As you think about the differences between religious groups, you soon realize it is their rules, beliefs, and themes that differentiate them. These themes guide the group members' actions and behaviors. These themes separate right from wrong. Without these themes, people might not have the need for different religions.

Ironically, when it comes to business, the concept of themes is relatively uncommon. Three elements drive most businesses: the passion, the market, and the leader's unique view. All three of these elements can differ dramatically from industry to industry, as well as among specific businesses. They are difficult to quantify and articulate. They also change dramatically over time. When a business owner introduces themes into the business's culture, the business improves; what's more, the owner helps the business create a life of its own.

Business themes are lenses that people can use to help themselves look at various situations and communicate the relative importance. Themes guide people in discerning right from wrong. They help create consistency by pulling individuals together as one. Put together, themes become a road map that helps a driver know where to turn or when to stop for fuel. Themes define a business and what it can become. As business owners begin to adopt these themes, they realize they cannot function effectively without them since the themes are essential to an organization's growth and health.

As I take you through an examination of each of the twelve business themes in the following chapters, try to understand them, not challenge them. Try to find relevance within them and add your own shades of color to them as they relate to your industry and business. You can read them as a complete series or reflect on individual themes and use them to take inventory within your own business. Whatever your method of processing these themes, through doing so, you will gain insights into your existing business, other successful business strategies, and the means of setting the foundation for growth.

Twelve Business
Themes for Growth

1. People:

PEOPLE ARE YOUR GREATEST ASSET

None of us is as smart as all of us.

—Ken Blanchard

People are your greatest asset: the five simple words of this theme are easy to understand, and most individuals can articulate what they think this statement means. However, of the many businesses I have observed over the years, few of their owners are successful in translating this simple theme into practice.

When I give talks, I ask people in the audience to use their own words to explain the meaning of this business theme. Often I hear statements such as "Without people, there is no business," "People are critical to the success of business," and "People are what it is all about!" To almost all my listeners it seems obvious that the most important element of this theme is people. This may even reflect your understanding too.

However, I want to focus on the last word: *asset.* According to *Webster's Dictionary*, an *asset* is "something desired ... something of value." This definition brings to mind a whole host of physical objects that people think of as important assets. The list might include an expensive vehicle or a piece of furniture that has been in the family for many generations. Most people would put a home on the list, and some would also include smaller items, such as jewelry, artwork, or books. People spend time and money to maintain their assets. When people have limited resources, they pay the most attention to their most important assets.

An *asset* is also defined as "an investment on which you hope to get a return." Unfortunately, for many business owners this alternate meaning of *asset* brings to mind a list of physical objects: buildings, company vehicles, office equipment, and the like. Most would also include people on this list, acknowledging that people are an essential component of a successful business. However, business owners typically lavish more of their resources on acquiring and maintaining physical assets. They simply do not see people as assets that require a high degree of attention. In the remodeling business, it is common for a business owner to treat tools and the employees who use them in the same way. In other words, the owner sees both as the means to accomplishing a task. Yet, we need to take care of and invest in people in a different way. Unlike mere tools, people can learn and grow. In fact, they need to learn and grow in order to progress along a defined path.

According to the experts, 85 percent of a business is made up of what folks commonly refer to as "intangible capital," most of which is its people. Most businesses will invest $10,000 to $20,000 in the first six months of a new employee's tenure, and, depending on his or her role, the cost of a team member leaving can be $100,000 or more. Don't take my word for it, though. Make a list of all of the expenses involved in finding or replacing an employee. Include the cost of recruiting possible hires and the value of everyone's time spent interviewing, checking references, and training the new team member. Next, do not forget about the expenses associated with finding an employee to temporarily fill in for someone who leaves, as well as the cost of communicating personnel changes to people both inside and outside your business. Finally, include the cost of lost opportunity, the work you were not able to undertake because you did not have the personnel.

The number you come up with will not be a trivial sum. This sum represents only one aspect of an employee's value. That person's creativity and intelligence, reliability and perseverance, and loyalty and dedication are much more difficult to put a price on. Despite that, these qualities are equally, if not more, valuable to a company's success.

The business owners who adopt this theme are much more successful than those who do not. Consider leaders of investment companies who are looking to invest: they assign a great deal of importance to the people, as assets, for whom they are paying, and the multiples for their evaluations are greater. Some major corporations have used the people-as-assets theme as part of a marketing campaign. One memorable example is the Verizon network ad campaign, which depicted a huge mass of people actually standing behind the Verizon spokesperson. In addition to highlighting speed, availability, and pricing, the ad places emphasis on the crowd of people who represent its network, which is an effective way for Verizon to differentiate itself from other telecoms. The crowd of people is a metaphor for the size and reach of the communications network; it is also an illustration of the number of people Verizon employs who support that network and, by inference, the customers who use its network. The ad's visual effect is memorable, at least in part because it presents the Verizon team as a real asset and a point of differentiation from the company's competition.

Your employees both fulfill the duties in their job descriptions and are recruiters for new talent. They make up your think tank, developing new products and services. They are brand builders, and they help with a critical part of your marketing strategy, which is attracting new clients. They are your grievance counselors when someone at the company experiences a personal loss or issue. Finally, they are company cheerleaders and morale boosters. They create a gung-ho environment that drives the rest of the team members to achieve better results.

As with any valuable asset, people's risks and liabilities are as great as the potential returns they provide. To get the best return, an employer must actively develop a level of mastery. However, unless the leader of a company invests in training and education, the value of that company's employee assets deteriorates. Unless people are given the means by which to grow and the opportunity in which to grow, they stagnate. If they are not given the opportunity to achieve, they grow restless or discontented. Not only does their work product suffer, but their attitude also changes for the worse. They may infect others on the team or leave the wrong impression with clients or vendors.

In any business, education occurs almost constantly through trial and error, or on-the-job training. Yet the lessons people learn in this haphazard way may not achieve the results you desire. The best approach to development comes from deliberate efforts made through organizing workshops, role-playing, outside coaches, and a variety of other means. Whatever the means you use, ensure that your effort receives the necessary resources for your company to succeed.

To realize the maximum benefit from adopting this theme, you must begin at the top by living according to it and demonstrating it through your actions. You could make investments through giving your time, training employees, and working with other tools to make your employees feel they are your greatest assets.

Remember, you cannot accomplish any improvement with understanding and love alone. Investing in assets requires time and money. Just how much time and money depends on your evaluation of where you stand now and your vision for where you want to go. Realize that for many businesses, including your own, implementing this theme can invoke a long-term cultural shift at the organization. To strengthen your resolve to stick with implementing the theme, try to quantify the projected returns. For example, imagine what the effect on your business would be if half your salespeople were to produce at rates 10 to 20 percent higher than they currently produce. Alternatively, use returns to calculate the savings you would accrue if you were able to reduce employee attrition.

From then on, as you budget for each new year, ask yourself how much you should be investing in your greatest assets to achieve these desired results. Remember too that your investment is not just financial; it involves your time and your energy, both of which are necessary to communicate critical ideas and continually reinforce them in your team.

Implementing this theme leads to immediate results, but it also begins to affect company culture by leading to long-term benefits and growth. You will improve the bottom line, and you will make your business a happier place. Begin with simply posting this theme on the wall of your office, noting it in your company newsletter, and placing flyers printed with it in all the mailboxes.

2. Commitment:

INVEST TIME TO IMPROVE

I don't think much of a man who is not
wiser today then he was yesterday.

—Abraham Lincoln

Our second theme is a close cousin to the first. In addition to addressing the current state of affairs, it also covers the commitment to constant improvement that is critical to future success and growth. Investing time to improve differentiates a good business from a great business.

We see this commitment to constant improvement every day in athletes' achievements. Athletes are never satisfied with their current accomplishments. They work constantly to improve, whether that means they are trying to gain a little more speed, strength, or agility. They strive constantly to push themselves to the limit and go faster, higher, and farther until they reach the natural limits imposed by age and anatomy.

However, a business has no such natural limitations. A five-year-old business can improve as much or as little as a twenty-five-year-old business can. A fifty-year-old business can be reinvented into an amazing platform for success. A business owner can overcome the limits of the marketplace by changing the company's "anatomy" and diversifying its offerings into different products and services.

Unfortunately, when things get a little tough in the business environment and expenses need to be cut, the typical business owner tends to reduce the amount of time and money invested in improvement and training. This is exactly the opposite of what should happen.

Recently, while facilitating a meeting among some larger remodeling businesses, I asked the company leaders to add up the number of hours they had invested in training individuals five years ago, when the business environment was very flush, as opposed to the amount of time they invested more recently, when the economy became much more challenging. The business owners whose companies had experienced positive growth in the last twelve months (about 20 percent of them) had all invested more time and money into training than they had five years ago. The ones who had experienced a decline or loss in annual sales were spending less time and money on training than they had five years ago. While this discussion covered a small sample of about twenty businesses, those businesses are fairly large and so their leaders are more likely than those of the average remodeling company to invest in improvement. This leads me to conclude that a similar poll among companies outside this group would yield results that were no better, and probably worse.

The theme of investing time to improve goes beyond the institutional activities of training. It really gets into the individual DNA of the folks you select for your team. Each of these people has a different skills profile and a varying need for improvement. Often, the most difficult team members to assess are those who are naturally skilled and talented. While it is fairly easy to tell when they are moving backward, it can be difficult to determine if they are moving forward or simply coasting. Even your top performers will become average if they are not investing time to improve themselves. In an effort to coach and nourish this process, you can toss them an improvement article from a magazine to read or an educational CD to listen to. If they grab the improvement gift and act on it, that is a positive sign. If, in contrast, they tell you they have not made the time to read or listen to your offering, that is one strike against them on their improvement scale. If you instill the theme of investing time to improve into overall communications and celebrate the successes that come from this theme, more of your team will buy into the benefits and get on board (if not, that is also a sign for required change). The best way for them to give themselves a raise is by improving.

Investing time to improve relates not just to employees but also to your company's client experiences, business processes, communication vehicles, and products and services. This theme is about with having an edge and developing the mindset of never being completely satisfied with current successes while always hungering for more. An extra 1 percent improvement is often the difference between winning and losing or between getting business or not. It is the difference between being good and being great. Each day, a business leader and his or her team members need to wake up asking, "Where can I invest time to improve?"

3. Mastery:

IF YOU GIVE, YOU GET

---

*No matter what accomplishments you
make, somebody helped you.*

—Althea Gibson

As a child, I was taught the importance of being charitable to others and unselfish, which means putting the needs of others before your own. However, over the years, I have discovered being unselfish and giving to others is also quite selfish and a key to both professional and personal growth. Think about the many elements of joy you received from giving, but also how you grew personally in the process. My first business experience with the power of unselfishness as a conscious strategy came early in my career. It began with an opportunity to speak on a variety of design and remodeling topics to the National Remodeling Association in the early 80's. Initially, I had some natural discomfort sharing my secrets and about public speaking. Yet, eventually, I found the experience forced me to take my understanding of the subject to a whole new level. By sharing my knowledge with others as I helped them, I simultaneously pushed my level of mastery and understanding of the subject matter to a higher level.

This initial speaking engagement led to many others that addressed different audiences from many business sectors. I gave one seminar to a consumer group on how to tackle home remodeling, and a local radio producer happened to be in the audience. After the seminar, the producer asked me if I had ever been on the radio. I had never even thought about it. He said he felt my method of communicating the topic of home remodeling could work in a radio-show format and invited me to audition at his radio station. As a result, I ended up hosting my own radio show on a top-ranked, local radio station for about ten years. That radio show did a great deal to advance our company's standing and brand in the local market, and it also helped to attract media attention that I, and our company, might otherwise not have received (all stemming from giving to others).

At our company I extended this experience and concept through the methods used to help team members with personal development. Thinking about the benefits I had experienced in sharing my knowledge with others and taking my professional game to the next level, I created a training environment in which our management team members had to share their knowledge with others through coaching and outside speaking. As expected, our leaders' proficiency and mastery of a variety of subjects increased dramatically, taking their personal skills to a higher level and raising the overall sophistication of our business. Plus, while developing presentations they could use to communicate with others, they discovered innovative ideas and approaches for everything from marketing to developing new products, services, and training techniques.

Some may think this series of events was just a coincidence or a product of dumb luck. That may be true, but I believe that this process of giving set the stage for whatever it is that we think of as *good luck*. When I think about the number of opportunities that our company has experienced since that time as a result of unselfish giving (or just putting myself in a context to give and help others learn and improve), the results reinforce the axiom, "if you give, you get" as a theme to use for growth.

So, how do you make this theme part of your business culture? Begin by changing your mindset. The next time you, as a representative of your company, are asked to speak to a group or participate in an event, think of speaking or another type of giving opportunity as a gift, not a distraction or obligation. Or the next time you are asked to assist a team member to increase his or her knowledge or proficiency, don't feel burdened. Think about what you or the business might learn from the experience and how you might leverage this opportunity. Identify others in your business who are passionate about a particular issue or subject (or just love to help others), and give them the opportunity to share their enthusiasm and knowledge. They will move heaven and earth to give to others and improve their value to the business too.

Eventually, this giving mindset will become a positive virus, of sorts, that spreads throughout your organization.

Remember, it is the *giving* that takes effort; the *getting* happens by itself. Avoid feelings of resentment if you do not receive immediate rewards for the efforts. It can be hard to feel motivated if you are constantly keeping score. Most of the time, in my experience, some knowledge or learning takes place. In the long run, these small acts of unselfishness accumulate and lead to huge and unforeseen benefits.

I believe that this theme is about growth, growth for those who receive the gift and for those who give, growth in new ideas and higher skills. It has the potential for the biggest impact on a company's bottom line and plays a major role in what direction an organization ultimately takes and what it becomes. As this theme becomes part of the company culture, the flow of giving opportunities becomes more regular and abundant.

4. Action:

LISTEN, LEARN, AND THEN RESPOND

---

*Even if you are on the right track, you'll
get run over if you just sit there.*

—Will Rogers

Most people's businesses are very well intended, but very few are successful. Why? One piece of the answer lies in how well informed the business is, and how consistently the business acts on what it learns.

Whenever I think about how we act or follow up on knowledge we have gained, two quotations come to mind. One comes from Ken Blanchard, the bestselling author and business guru, who coined the phrase, "Intentions minus actions equals squat." This statement is an amusing yet powerful reminder that we are all guilty of inaction. Great ideas become meaningless unless we do something with them. The second quotation is a proverb: "The road to hell is paved with good intentions." The word *hell* could be replaced with *failure* and the proverb would have a better business application. Remember business *success* is a verb, not a noun.

"Listen, learn, and then respond" speaks to issues that businesses face every day. This theme reminds us that before we act, we need to be receptive to the situation around us, understand what the real problems are, and plan our actions accordingly. Business owners need to listen in a variety of ways. A business leader needs to listen to the overall market, clients, business partners, and team members. Sometimes listening can take the form of a casual, ear-to-the-ground approach. At other times, it calls for more formal measures, such as implementing surveys and focus groups. Either way, this listening must be active. It must be deliberate and focused, and it must be given the highest priority in every interaction. Only then, through such active listening, can we leaders hope to learn enough to be able to act.

An example of how this theme works took place when our company's business was growing very rapidly several years ago. I began to notice that the distance between our craftsmen and our senior leadership team was growing. This was not simply due to the fact that there were more unfamiliar faces, although that was certainly the case. Instead, other managers and I were hearing more "us-versus-them" comments, as well as more questioning of important business decisions. While this may have been a natural product of the company's growth, it was not a good dynamic. Through listening to what this situation was telling me and other managers, together we recognized that a gap in communications was the culprit. Employees who worked in the field felt disconnected from the decision makers, while people in management were so focused on their own piece of the rapidly changing picture that they lost perspective regarding how their decisions were affecting the rest of the company.

At the same time my team and I realized cellphone use was becoming the norm among employees in the office and the field. Based on this observation, we decided to launch a program that came to be known as Case in a Minute. This program amounted to a simple sixty-second message sent to every Case team member via cellphone every Thursday at 5 pm. This message included an update on sales or marketing trends, reminders for upcoming events, and simple celebrations of successes by individual team members.

Through our commitment to listening to what was happening in our business environment, my team members and I learned about both the underlying causes of problems and the potential solutions. When we acted on what we had learned, a great thing happened. Case in a Minute kept people informed. Plus, the program restored employees' connection to company leadership; it has become an integral part of the business's internal communication system. In fact, it expanded to our national business and to the company's key communication strategy. Even some members of our business alliances have adopted this simple tool and leveraged it to one hundred times the scale we have.

Another practical application of this theme came through the launch of our national business. In the mid-1990s the successful launch of our local handyman division received some national media attention. As a result, the company began to get calls from remodelers and builders from around the country asking if our team members could help them launch similar handyman divisions for their businesses. In a short time the inquiries went from one per month to one per day.

We could have shrugged off these calls easily as flattering distractions, but, fortunately, we were listening and realized that the market was receptive to a national business model. We organized a think tank made up of internal and external advisors to explore our options and determine the level of energy it would take to launch a national business. Once the timing was right, we flipped the switch. By actively listening to our market and then responding to opportunity, we created a national franchise business.

The key to success with this theme is twofold: first, you must observe and understand what is occurring in the circumstances around you; second, you must be able to see the connections among these occurrences. This leads naturally to sound decisions and effective actions that create intended outcomes. Again, with listening, learning, and responding, success and growth will follow.

5. Experience:

BUSINESS IS ABOUT THE EXPERIENCE

Why wait to become memorable?

—Tony Robbins

If you ask a client what it was that caused him or her to contact your company, you will hear something like, "I need to fix my entry door," "I want to buy a sofa," or "I need a caterer for my daughter's graduation party." People will tell you about a specific product or service they require, or they will describe some problem they need to solve, or some pain they need to eliminate.

Similarly, if you ask your team members to describe the business your company is in, you will hear the same kind of answer: the remodeling business, the retail furniture business, or the food service business. In fact, you yourself would probably answer the question in the same way. That is because your passion for, and interest in, your business is defined in your mind by a specific product or service.

If you, your team members, and your clients all consistently think about your business in terms of the product or service provided, it is only natural to believe that the product or service is, in fact, what the business is all about, and that the company's success will be based on the ability to deliver the product or service very well.

Your business's success does depend on the ability to deliver a great product or service, but that kind of competence is a given. What your clients will remember is the experience of doing business with your company. In fact, they will remember the experience long after the product or service you provided is forgotten.

Over the years, our remodeling business has received hundreds of letters from clients after we completed projects for them. Very few of the clients make any mention of a window's energy efficiency or the tight seams in a room's crown molding. Instead, these letters address the experiences clients had while we were doing remodeling for them. I remember one client going on and on about how our carpenter unselfishly shoveled her driveway to help her get to work on time the morning after a snowstorm. Another client highlighted the two hours our project manager spent going around the neighborhood and helping her find her lost dog. Letter after letter told a similar story. Eventually, we began to realize that the final product did not hold a candle to the experiences we created in our clients' lives while providing that product.

But what do I mean when I say that the experience is important? Let us look at the elements involved. The first is communication. If you are competent at your craft, but you still have problems with your clients, poor communication is the most likely reason. How and when you communicate with clients will dramatically affect their experiences.

Many years ago my team members and I were in the final stages of a kitchen project for a doctor who was very focused on the construction's details. We needed to replace two cabinet doors that had flaws in the wood finish, and our project manager had scheduled a few hours in an afternoon to complete the work. After installing one door, our top carpenter realized that the other door was incorrect. He left the original door in place and called the project manager, reporting the need to reorder the door and scheduling a return to the house when it arrived. The project manager decided he would explain this situation to the client the next day during his regular visit to the site.

That night, when the client arrived home, he was completely unaware of what had transpired. He anxiously went to look at the work that he assumed had been completed that day and was pleased to see the new cabinet door. Then, he was shocked to find the other door had not been replaced. Not only was he disappointed, but he also began making a list of all the other little details that, in his mind, were not perfect. That night, he sat down and wrote a lengthy e-mail addressed to several members of our team in which he referred to the workers as "incompetent" and "dishonest" because he felt they had tried to hide things from him. Thus, a satisfied client became a deeply dissatisfied client simply because a project manager had postponed a simple communication.

Communication needs to be clear, and it needs to occur at the right time. How you communicate is often as important as what you communicate. Every client differs in how he or she wants to receive information (in terms of how often and in what degree of detail), so being a little flexible is important. Remember, a client's memories will be based on the experience as well as the product or service.

Another element of a great customer experience is going beyond expectations to deliver something extra. The examples of snow shoveling and helping to search for a lost dog, which I described above, fit the bill. One of those client letters I mentioned earlier focused on how our carpenters had gone above and beyond the job requirements and provided an extra set of belt hooks in the master bedroom closet; those hooks cost next to nothing, but they raised the customer satisfaction score from a nine to a ten.

As a business owner, you must establish this kind of extra effort as a core value within your company. Every team member needs to be empowered to do whatever it takes to solve a client's problem and make it an extraordinary experience. This process can get expensive, so it helps to define certain limits. At the Ritz-Carlton, for example, frontline employees have authorization to spend over a thousand dollars to solve a guest's problem without having to check with management first. Whatever limits you set, your team members should understand how to recognize an opportunity to provide something extra, while having the authority to act on those opportunities should be part of the business culture.

A third element of this theme concerns how problems are handled, regardless of what those problems may be. In the remodeling business, for example, sometimes an employee's work does not meet with a client's or supervisor's approval. The natural tendency, then, is for a craftsman or a designer to defend the work and actions because of his or her passion. Often, however, this defensiveness just makes the situation worse. A better approach is to recognize that the criticism may have nothing to do with the work product per se. Instead, the issue may have more to do with client expectations, failure to communicate, or any number of causes. If the employee can begin to listen and look at situations less defensively and personally and to thereby address the process and the product in a rational manner, the likelihood for an improved client experience is dramatically better.

If business owners focus on the delivery of a wonderful experience as much as on the delivery of a quality product or service, success will be significantly higher.

6. Planning:

IF YOU FAIL TO PLAN, THEN PLAN TO FAIL

It's a dream until you write it down; then it becomes a goal.

—Anonymous

Imagine a pilot flying from New York to Los Angeles without a flight plan. Not only would the arrival time be uncertain, the plane might end up in San Francisco after being exposed to a pretty bumpy ride through a storm system. Flight plans are essential to flying safely; they help pilots to avoid dangerous weather and other air traffic. In addition to helping pilots stay on course, they also help set expectations for traffic controllers and others on related support teams. For this reason, flight plans are not optional; they are an automatic part of both commercial and recreational flying processes.

The important message in terms of business here is making the development of a flight plan the rule. If you really believe not having a plan will result in something bad, it is not optional. If you believe you will fail in business if you do not have a plan, you will have the conviction and ability to invest the time, becoming proficient at planning and developing the discipline to create plans before you act.

Planning is an essential business skill that all business owners need to perfect if they want to compete and be successful. Planning needs to be part of a company's DNA. It is a prerequisite for all discussions and decision-making processes.

Although all business owners agree about the importance of planning, most are not as proficient at it as they need to be. As I have studied businesses within different industries, I have found that in different market conditions, the employees' commitment to planning and the planning process changes if that commitment is not ingrained in the organization's culture. In a tough economy, for example, many business leaders abandon long-term planning and become totally focused on the short term. Such leaders are like pilots who are so focused on a local weather system that they forget about the ultimate goal of arriving at their destination on time and about the traffic pattern ahead. In business, as in flight, every adjustment needs both to respond to the immediate problem or unexpected obstacle and to keep the end result in mind. When a business's leaders commit to planning as a core activity or theme, it is much easier for them to respond to changing business conditions without abandoning their long-term vision for the company.

One way to frame this more pragmatically is to think about the percentage of time a business's leaders are focused on short-, medium-, and long-term planning. In normal conditions, for example, a leadership team may spend one-third of its planning time on each. When the economy gets tough and there is more of a scarcity in sales, the business leaders may need to devote 75 percent of planning time to the short-term, 20 percent to the medium-term, and 5 percent to the long-term. You can debate the percentages, but the importance of keeping leaders' eyes on all three time frames is critical.

The flip side triggers a similar dynamic. Some businesses are entirely too focused on the long-term. In fact, they are so focused on mapping out long-term plans that they stumble on short-term activities. A friend's grandfather used to tell him, "Just fill the wagon and don't worry about the mule going blind." Finding the right balance can be tricky, but it gets easier as you gain mastery of the planning process and mindset.

Planning has many dimensions of proficiency. First, business leaders need to be excellent at immediate short-term planning. Norman Vincent Peale famously said, "Plan your work today and every day, and then work your plan." Again, planning is not an occasional or optional task. Successful people have heightened planning skills that they employ on a daily basis. They realize they can accomplish much more if they make the planning process an integral part of each day. This process also allows them to build in appointments with themselves for medium- and long-term planning activities.

Planning also needs to be part of what everyone at the company does on a daily basis. If a salesperson says she intends to sell three projects that month, the leader's first reaction should be this: "Great. What's your plan?" The leader should not start doing a victory dance before feeling comfortable there is a solid plan in place. If the sales associate does not have a plan, the leader should discount the likelihood of sales. If a project manager says a project will be completed in thirty days, the supervisor's response should be, "Let's see the plan or flow chart that will show the milestones that allow the goal to be achieved." These reactions should become automatic and part of everyone's normal behavior.

If an organization's leaders and employees fully embrace this theme, all of the people connected to that organization improve in planning, as a skill, and also become more committed to the discipline required to become masterful at this skill.

7. Expectations:
EXCEED EXPECTATIONS

It never gets easier; you just go faster.

—Greg LeMond

For many years I worked with a fellow named Bill Millholland. Bill is a very creative, extremely talented designer. Whenever I was seeking that magical graphic idea to add to a presentation, I tap Bill on the shoulder. Typically, I share my overall goal, without wasting a great deal of time explaining all of my ideas, and then let him run with it. Given his passion and interest in this area, generally he is happy and willing to help. I usually suggest that we meet again in a couple of days so as not to be too disruptive to his priorities and schedule. However, Bill consistently sends me a note the following day, asking for a time to meet and to share some of his thoughts. Wow! I always marvel that he is ahead of schedule. Bill exceeds my expectations. When we meet, without fail, he showed me something that always exceeds my expectations. He presents cool graphic ideas and even goes further to make suggestions about language.

This experience is not infrequent. It happens every time I work with Bill. How does this make me feel? Wonderful.

Because Bill always exceeds my expectations, I do not have to spend time explaining my ideas in detail. I do not have to follow up and remind him of anything, and I do not have the cloud of that project hanging over my head. Instead, I can turn my energy and focus on other things, and I can accomplish more. I can make promises and deliver my presentation to the printer early. All of this happens because Bill consistently exceeds expectations.

Exceeding expectations has the same effect on your clients. It transforms them into raving fans. For example, in the remodeling business, if a client asks when you expect to complete the project and you tell him or her it will be done by Thursday, you set up the possibility for one of three common outcomes. The first is you are late (even if it is just by one day, you are still late). The client is disappointed, and he or she may begin to lose trust in you, which may affect future opportunities. Finishing a project late adds stress and requires you to waste additional time explaining and making excuses. You will probably lose money because of this inefficiency or potential lost opportunities with other clients.

What about the other outcomes? The second scenario is finishing on time. Finishing on time is much better than being late, but you should not expect any high fives from the client for being on time. The third outcome is to exceed expectations and finish early. This outcome will earn you ten times the benefits of merely being on time. The client will be ecstatic. A happy client will pay you promptly and gladly recommend your company to friends and colleagues. This client is now a raving fan, which moves your business relationship to a higher level.

Exceeding expectations should not just be a one-off experience; it should be a business strategy. This theme is not simply related to an individual dynamic. If your company consistently exceeds expectations in all elements of the business, the benefits accumulate. The business grows by word-of-mouth referrals, which could result in reduced marketing expenses. The business becomes a desirable place of employment, which could lead to greater retention of existing employees and reduced training and recruitment expenses. The business is thus better positioned to grow and you are able to invest more time in long-term thinking, rather than wasting effort constantly putting out fires. Overall, the business will become a much healthier, happier place.

Implementing this theme seems easy, but it is not. I have found that consistently exceeding expectations takes individual and collective courage. Business people tend to be "pleasers," acquiescing to each client's wishes or goals. Unless you and everyone on your team understand how to set initial expectations, it is easy for a client to push for an unrealistic expectation that cannot be exceeded and, even worse, cannot be met. If you want to make exceeding expectations a theme by which your company can grow, you need to begin training your employees to communicate with courage and conviction. Creating this type of environment requires making sure the right people are in the right positions. Otherwise, the likelihood of exceeding expectations is dramatically reduced. While developing a culture of exceeding expectations should be a goal coming out of the gate when you start your business, this theme can only be perfected when you and your team members' passion and competency are properly aligned.

8. Communication:

IT IS OUR OBLIGATION TO COMMUNICATE, NOT THE RESPONSIBILITY OF OTHERS TO UNDERSTAND

The difference between the right word and almost the right word is the difference between lightning and a lightning bug.

—Mark Twain

Every day, we are bombarded with communication. We spend huge amounts of time and energy communicating in both our personal and professional lives. We teach our children to use their words, not their fists. We have even created positions in business with titles such as communications director to address the virtually constant need to communicate. The irony is that even with all this, communication remains one of the biggest challenges in life and in business.

Miscommunication results in divorce, waste, and even war. Roughly 90 percent of all business challenges result from miscommunication. Miscommunication can cost a business more money than any other type of error.

In the Internet age, the problem of miscommunication is compounded by communication's increased speed and volume. With e-mail, text messaging, and tweets becoming prevalent as the primary ways by which many people communicate, mastery of these new communication tools has become more important than ever. In fact, many businesses have introduced proper etiquette training for the use of these technological communication tools. Even though such instant-reaction communication techniques have created greater efficiency and transparency, they have also increased the probability of miscommunication.

The key to understanding this theme is realizing that it is not actually about communication. Instead, the theme is really about ownership and accountability. Who owns the communication? Consider these questions: Is the pitcher or the catcher responsible for getting the ball thrown over the plate? Is the hammer or the nail responsible for sinking into the wood? Who owns the communication: the person delivering it or the person receiving it?

In answering the last question, if you agree up front (rather than after the miscommunication occurs) that the deliverer of the communication owns it and is accountable, you dramatically reduce the number of misunderstandings that occur.

The idea of *ownership* is overused in business conversation, but it applies particularly well in this case. When I own a home, I care for it differently than I would if I rented it. As a homeowner, I spend more time thinking about my home. I am more concerned with maintenance and repair, and I protect my home from abuse. As a homeowner, I look at the consequences of both my short- and long-term decisions, and I see my home as an investment, not just an expense. If you can begin to think about ownership of communication in this way, you will both reduce your chances of miscommunication and create an environment that has a much higher degree of trust.

An example may help to illustrate the power of this theme. Imagine you have a craftsman renovating the dining room in your home. He has installed a 2.5-inch chair rail to add some interest and detailing to the room. As you are viewing his handiwork, you ask if adding a crown molding would make sense and would complement the chair rail. As a professional craftsman, he acknowledges that this makes sense. He also asks if you would prefer a 3- or 5-inch crown molding. Given your limited knowledge about moldings, your only basis for answering him is the 2.5-inch chair rail. Since the chair rail looks good, you conclude that the 3-inch crown molding will work well.

The craftsman writes an addendum to your contract and orders and buys the material. Two weeks later, he begins to install the new crown molding. When he's almost finished, you walk into the room. Immediately, you notice that the crown molding looks skimpy. It does not have the same generous scale the chair rail has. When you interrupt the craftsman to discuss the matter, he remarks that the crown molding he is installing is the size on which you agreed. He reminds you that he gave you a choice between the 3-inch and 5-inch crown molding.

Who is at fault here? We could debate the degree to which both parties share in the miscommunication. However, no matter what arguments we make, it will be an expensive miscommunication for the craftsman. He has lost time, possibly three to five hours, has an unhappy client, and also may experience some frustration and loss of pride in his carpentry work.

If the craftsman had really understood what it meant to *own* his communication, he would have gone overboard in making sure the client understood the possible choices. In minutes, he could have explained how the crown was installed at an angle, which made it look smaller than its dimension implied. He could have asked a few questions to judge how much the client knew about molding or to ascertain her priorities. He could have grabbed a piece of wood of similar size to illustrate the scale of the two different sizes. In fact, there were many simple ways by which the craftsman could have avoided this miscommunication. However, none of them would have been available to him until he had learned to take ownership of the communication.

Imagine if everyone in your organization were to fully adopt this theme. It would result in more delighted clients, fewer mistakes, more profit, less stress, and an overall healthier and fitter business.

9. Relationships:

CREATE CLIENTS AND BUSINESS WILL FOLLOW

Good counselors lack no clients.

—William Shakespeare

Most business owners and team members believe that if you do business (that is, provide a product or service for payment) with someone, that someone then becomes a client. While this is obvious and true, if you reverse the order of this statement and truly create a client first, you have the beginning of a powerful business and growth strategy.

Think of a potential client as someone who has not yet paid you for your product or services. How many potential clients does your business have? In some businesses, the number may be one out of ten; in others it may be one out of a hundred. However, in all businesses, your present client base is much less than your potential client base. You do not have to take this exercise very far before you realize that the number of prospects for your products or services is huge. It may, in fact, be ten, one hundred, or even one thousand times the number of paying clients you have at present.

Why wait for someone to do business with you before you treat and consider him or her as a client? How do you interact with a client versus a nonclient? Is your reaction time or willingness to address that person's pain the same? Imagine how it might change the way you interact and communicate with people if you treated them all like clients before they started doing business with you. Many things would change. Your messaging would be more about them and their needs than about you and your company. You would connect to many more people in a more sincere, meaningful way because you would see them as friends, rather than strangers.

For some, this mindset takes a little time to adopt. I began to think this way early in my career. For me, this mindset was somewhat natural because of my upbringing. My parents encouraged me to help others, because doing so was and is always the right thing to do. While it was not strategic at first, I began to see substantial results whenever I adopted this point of view. If you make your core purpose helping others in a sincere and meaningful way, everyone who might need your product and service becomes a client. They feel this level of care and attention, and this helpful mindset differentiates your company from other business leaders who are simply trying to push a product or service. Eventually, I began to think of this concept as a business theme and a growth strategy. I found that by making everyone in our company more disciplined in this approach, our results improved.

Most businesses and sales organizations put an enormous amount of time and energy into presenting their products and services. They develop marketing and sales strategies to get someone to buy today. They develop tools and lengthy presentations about their product or service to convince the client to buy from their company rather than from a competitor. Very quickly, the interaction becomes mostly about the business and not much about the prospective client. Many clients find this approach offensive; they put up defensive barriers early and eventually stop listening.

If, instead, you turn your focus on the prospective client and away from your product or service, you will change the dynamic of the relationship. If your first priority is genuinely to try to help the potential client any way you can, you are treating that person like a client, not just a prospect, and you will see a very different outcome. For example, a prospect may call you to discuss renovating a bathroom. In the course of getting to know him or her, you may realize the prospect may need help with refinancing a home or finding help with childcare. If you believe in creating clients so that business will follow, you help any way you can. Although most people do not contact a business with the idea of developing a new friendship, most prospects will appreciate and respond to members of an organization who do not merely try to sell them something.

So, how does this approach change things? First, client-centered relationships require time. If you are going to help people, you need to understand them and their context better. The initial conversation you or a team member has with a caller is only secondarily about setting an appointment. The primary goal is to understand the caller's needs and to begin to think about how you or someone else at the company can best guide that caller.

Second, this approach requires that you devote most of your initial interaction to listening, not talking. The more you understand, the more you can properly guide the prospect. I am not referring to passive listening; instead, I refer to active engagement. You need to probe into what people tell you to uncover all of the factors that have prompted them to come to you in the first place and that may hold the key to your being able to satisfy them.

Finally, you must be ready to lose the prospective business and even to advise a prospect not to do business with you. This does not mean you have lost a client, however. In fact, many people will remember how well you treated them and will come back to you, if not for the original reason, then for future needs. I know it seems counterintuitive, but if you are truly living by this theme, you will receive an abundance of opportunities that will lead to new business.

As you and your team members begin to adopt this theme as part of your business culture, you also will gain a new perspective of yourselves. Your sales people will seem more like therapists than sales representatives, and your production staff will look more like tour guides than craftsmen. Remember, this theme takes effect without your having to change anything about your product or service. You need only alter the way you and your team members think about your company's relationship with customers and the interactions with them. The result of this new perspective is that your company will become a magnet for the right kind of clients, and you will start to see positive results almost immediately.

In living by this theme, you will accomplish three things at your organization. First, you will improve your ability to provide good advice. Second, you will bind your team together in a more positive manner. This mindset will begin to filter into the interaction team members have with each other. The synergy and power of your team members becomes much greater when it is for the right reasons. Third, you will differentiate yourself and your business from your competitors. If you have five competitors arm wrestling for a client's business, most of them will be focused on traditional selling, not helping others first.

As with many of the themes I discuss in this book, this idea involves inherent contradictions that may make it, as an approach, difficult to implement. However, if you yourself begin by living according to this theme and then begin quantifying and celebrating the results, over time the pendulum will begin to shift.

10. Synergy:
ONE PLUS ONE EQUALS THREE

When you look at the sun, you see no shadows.

—Helen Keller

No, the title of this section is is not a trick or a mathematical error. It is a way of thinking in business and in life, and it is also a practical methodology by which you can create solutions that are otherwise not easily found.

"One plus one equals three" describes *synergy*, a condition in which the whole is greater than the sum of its parts. Synergistic thinking and methods need to be applied consistently as a process for you to really experience the benefits at your company. An example will make this easier to understand.

Many years ago, my team members and I were looking for creative ways to thank our remodeling clients. We wanted to do something that would be meaningful, create a nice memory, and leave people with a positive impression. While visiting a job site, I was talking about this idea with a craftsman who had just completed a deck for the client. As we were standing there, we noticed scraps of leftover decking materials waiting to be hauled away. We also noticed a children's play area in the yard. The carpenter suggested we build something with the scraps for the client's young child. We began to brainstorm what might be practical and also create a smile on the family members' faces. We came up with the idea for a children's picnic table. It was unique, only took about one hour to build, and was a great use of the extra decking materials. Building picnic tables (or something similar, utilizing leftover materials) became a standard part of our process of project completion. Even some clients' neighbors requested little tables, which became a tangible signature of our craft and of the clients' experiences too.

The theme of one plus one equals three in this case combined the ideas of a designer and a craftsman to address an issue or opportunity. The solutions the team came up with together were better and greater than anything they each would have created on their own.

While this theme can create some magical and spontaneous solutions, it can also be instituted as a calculated improvement process. Many years ago, Toyota implemented the Kaizen Process of Continuous Improvement. Using it, company leaders examine existing products and processes, and then they invest time to achieve incremental improvement.

I have personally experienced this process several times as a result of my company's partnership with Pella Windows. Pella is committed to constant improvement. On a regular basis, Pella leaders will assemble a group of individuals from different disciplines within the company—line workers, managers, and office staff—into Kaizen groups. Each of these groups is tasked with improving a particular product or process within the company. The group members follow a process that moves from deconstruction of the product or process to suggestions for reconstruction. The outcomes must include measurable levels of improvement. I have seen cases in which these groups have improved product performance by 30 percent while reducing costs by 20 percent. The process's success extends beyond improving a product or process to improving customer satisfaction. I have seen cases in which the client experience rating has significantly improved as a result of using the Kaizen strategy.

As you think about how to introduce the idea of synergy into your company culture, recognize that some people have an aptitude for this kind of thinking and some do not. Everyone can improve on the ability to think synergistically, but it helps to have some champions. One approach is to deliberately bring unlike parts and people together to interact, watch for the results, and celebrate any synergy that emerges. Be patient, since the participants may not see the benefit at first. Some of the most powerful results will come in mysterious ways.

Members of my team and I experienced this when we launched a bath division within our business by using a synergistic process. I brought together a group of employees from design, marketing, and production, and we laid out the opportunity and challenge together. As a result, this unique group developed a business model that grew to become a

$10 million division in just a few years. The success of this division was built on the synergy that came from people in different disciplines working together. The solutions and end result were far better than anything we would have conceived individually.

Participating in this process also brought out the best in people, sometimes surprisingly so. For example, the most soft-spoken, reluctant participator—a production manager—turned out to be the most important contributor. Through this process, we also identified an unexpected individual who could lead the charge and grow this part of business. His passion became clear during the process, and we handed him the responsibility of taking this aspect of the business to a new level. A fundamental belief in, and a commitment to, the synergistic process allowed all these people and ideas to come together.

As with many themes, it may take time to get some employees feeling comfortable with this type of interaction. However, as more and more people become comfortable with it, this interaction can spread and become a means of generating new ideas and ways to improve and grow the business.

11. Pace:
AGGRESSIVE BUT REALISTIC

---

*Things may come to those that wait, but they
are things left by those that hustle.*

—Abraham Lincoln

Do you ever get frustrated when a goal or task is not completed in the time frame you were expecting? This could be as simple as when someone arrives late for an appointment or as complex as a project going well beyond the original schedule. We do not think about the flip side as much, but it can also be disconcerting when something is delivered too early or completed well ahead of schedule.

When something does not happen as expected, people have a natural tendency to point fingers and blame others. We also tend to assume that a breakdown in communication is at the root of the problem. As discussed earlier, poor communication can cause many problems, but sometimes it is merely the vehicle, not the root cause. Often, the issue may actually be a matter of pace or cadence.

In sports, achieving the right pace can be the difference between winning and losing. We see this in track and cycling, sports in which athletes very carefully monitor not only average speeds but also heart rate, oxygen uptake, and calories burned. Pace is also important in a NASCAR race, where being in the lead is not merely a matter of physical position in the race but is also a function of the need to make a pit stop to refuel or change tires.

None of this behind-the-scenes science is clearly visible to the casual observer, who assumes that athletes' artful movements are attributable to their raw talent. Not to belittle the power of raw talent, but as levels of mastery increase, the balance between art and science begins to shift. Understanding science and the discipline to make this knowledge part of the performance becomes a much bigger factor of athletes' work and training because it can be measured and controlled.

Business has the same need for mastery, along with many factors that make that mastery difficult to achieve. Because of these variables, business leaders need to understand what a proper pace or cadence looks and feels like, and then they need to make it a part of the organization's culture.

How does one articulate *cadence*? For example, if you ask avid golfers how long a round of golf should take, they can give you an answer that is generally accurate to within a few minutes. Similarly, competitive cyclists can tell you within one or two beats per minute what the ideal heart rate would be for a twenty-mile time trial. Business leaders need to be able to answer their challenges with the same certainty. One way to do that is by making the concept of *pace* a priority within business culture.

The best way I have found to communicate what I mean by *pace* is to think about something as aggressive but realistic. The idea applies in almost all settings. You want your team members to be aggressive—that is, they should work hard, have an edge, and do the best they can with the resources at hand. However, this aggressive posture must be tempered with realism. If you are not realistic, being aggressive may work against you when you are trying to meet deadlines or attempting to be in sync with others. Being *realistic* means taking into account other priorities and evaluating them against the number of hours in the day (and fear of burning out), while also ensuring quality control. If you are so aggressive that you may have to redo something, the result can be more frustrating than being a little late would have been.

How does the theme of aggressive but realistic change your interactions with your team members? It plays a big role when you are discussing schedules and timelines. For instance, if a team member comes to you and says she hopes to have a project completed by the end of the week, you can ask, "Is that aggressive but realistic?" The team member now has a new filter through which to evaluate the answer. What about the other priorities for a project, such as the time allotted or the level of effort needed to achieve the desired quality? Instead of telling you what you want to hear, the team member will stop to rethink the matter, eventually providing you with one of three results. First, she may confirm that the original plan is aggressive but realistic. Second, she may become more realistic and ask for more time. Third, she may conclude that the original approach was not aggressive enough and she can get it done early if certain conditions are present (a quick price from the office, reassignment of personnel for a limited time, and so on).

This same filter can be used to gain alignment on many other aspects of your business. If a team member approaches you with a financial investment regarding a piece of real estate, you can simply ask if what you would be paying is aggressive but realistic. Alternatively, if a subcontractor gives you a bid with terms including time and available resources, you can ask if what is being proposed is aggressive but realistic.

By asking your team members to look at their work through this filter of what is aggressive but realistic, you foster dialogue and can create an opportunity for alignment on what the right pace or cadence might be for the task at hand. This may sound a little mechanical, but with some trial and error, you will discover that the answers you get when you pose this question are more diverse than you would think, and that some individuals fall more frequently in one answer category or another.

You must communicate pace every day with family, clients, team members, and alliance members, especially when major growth initiatives are involved. By incorporating this theme into your life culture, you encourage people to ask the right questions. That introduces more variety into the decision-making process, leading to better answers, better alignment, and higher profits.

One of the challenges you will face is making this theme part of everyone else's daily mantra. Begin by discussing the importance of finding the right cadence and explaining the consequences of misalignment. Then, make pace a priority in all of your communications. As with mastery in athletics, the desired cadence will eventually become second nature and part of the organization's success habits as practiced by team members.

12. Success:

DEFINING SUCCESS

ON TIME + ON BUDGET + DELIGHTED

CLIENT = SUCCESS

Success demands singleness of purpose.

—Vince Lombardi

Throughout all of our lives we have been given different definitions of *success*. In school our teachers start the year by sharing their grading system and criteria for a successful semester. Our doctors set a target weight or blood pressure that, in turn, sets the standard for success in our health. Finally, in sports, everyone agrees that the standard pretty much comes down to winning and losing.

Occasionally, though, someone may suggest a new definition of *success*. A coach might say, "It's not whether we win or lose; it's how we play the game," or "If you played your hardest, you should be proud and feel successful." It is clear, then, that *success* does not have a single definition, even within the same discipline. This is as true in business as in any other aspect of our lives.

The proof of this is that if you were to ask five key individuals in your business to write down what defines a successful month or year for the organization, you would probably get three or four different answers. The definitions will vary based on each person's worldview and perspective, and the exercise will be much harder and take much longer than you would expect.

Imagine what would happen to a sports team's performance if each player defined *success* differently. One player might define *success* as scoring as many points as possible while another might want only enough points to win. A third person might believe that *success* means staying healthy and getting to the next round, while a fourth might promote a win-at-all-costs mentality. All of them will approach the game with a different strategy and pace, and none of their beliefs may align with what the coach has in mind. Though short-term performance may not be affected, the long-term result is most likely a disaster.

In business, some believe success is all about profit, while others believe it is all about the client experience. While the lack of alignment is troublesome, it is not the fault of the individuals; more likely, it is a leadership problem. The best success formulas are a blend of holistic criteria— that is, they address the clients' experiences, the company's profit, short- and long-term issues, and individuals as well as the overall team. Many years ago we began discussing this subject at our company as it related to specific remodeling clients and projects. We wrote down adjectives that described positive, successful results. We realized that for a project to be considered successful, the process, the client's happiness, and the financial results needed to work in tandem. Finding the common denominator, while not easy, was and remains critical to bringing everyone closer to the same target. The formula we agreed upon was this: "On time + on budget + delighted client = success." This not only became a great rallying cry, but also gave us a more consistent way of celebrating and rewarding behavior and results. Prior to sharing this theme, some individuals would do a victory dance after beating a budget by 5 percent, despite missing the project deadline by two weeks and creating a frustrating client experience.

Each leg of the formula has multiple dimensions that can help to guide team members. "On time" means keeping promises and also speaks to the best use of the business's resources. Just like a football team's members who know when the snap is coming, sales and production team members operate efficiently and effectively only when everything is on time and in sync.

The second element, "on budget," is about more than net profit. It means accurately predicting and properly preparing for the expected results. It would be tough for any business to endure if project budgeting was a roll of the dice.

The third piece of the formula is "delighted client." Every day, our team members have numerous interactions with our clients, each of which is an opportunity to "check the pulse" of the client's happiness. A craftsman often judges the project's success based on high standards of workmanship, but clients react based on their feelings about the experience of the project, whether their comfort was compromised, and whether their expectations were met. Creating a "delighted client" is an important short-term goal; doing so also pays dividends down the road in referrals, repeat business, and reduced marketing expenses.

This formula, while simple, requires discussion and training. Once you believe everyone understands it, use the formula as a criterion when discussing projects and clients. You might ask a project manager, "Is the client delighted? How do you know? Have you done anything that was unexpected and exceeded his expectations? Has he referred friends to us?" While this may sound like a grilling, these questions help employees become conditioned to developing delighted clients. The same type of discussion should take place with the concepts of "on time" and "on budget."

More often than not, one of these three elements will achieve a very high score while the others will need some attention. It may not take much effort to bring the three into alignment—by spending a little more time analyzing project costs, reworking the schedule, or rethinking procurement—but all three must be in alignment for you to say that a project was truly successful.

Every business leader will have a different success formula based not only on the company's products and services but also on the organization's basic culture and the business owner's and leadership's goals. With everyone singing off the same sheet of music, profits will improve, the team members will respect each other more, and new business growth will follow.

Theme Summary

It is not hard to make decisions when
you know what your values are.

—Roy Disney

At the most successful businesses, themes become part of the company DNA and the puzzle pieces that together describe who they are. They are both a mindset and way of thinking. Together, they make up a formula that can be used to address any situation. They can shed light on an otherwise confusing decision. Eventually, company members need not even discuss them because they become a daily success routine. Fully understanding these themes may take minutes for some and years for others. Implementing these themes can be equally easy or complex. Some themes may be already in place at your company, but you never really realized they were "business themes for growth" until you heard them articulated this way. Some will take years to embrace, but you will encounter a moment when that theme becomes especially relevant and important based on a situation or business condition. Before the themes ever become meaningful to your business, these concepts start with you, the business leader. The process begins with your commitment and belief in these themes before your business, through yourself and your team members, can ever integrate or leverage them and bring them to life.

Bring Your Business Themes to Life

Success is a verb.

—Dan Kennedy

Many of you may remember a movie from 1984 titled *The Karate Kid.* In this movie, a student wants a master to teach him the art of karate so he can compete and, equally important, so he can protect himself at his new school. The student wants to jump in and learn specific moves, such as kicks and punches, on the first day. In what is a puzzling action for the student, the master hands the student a paintbrush and has him paint the fence, using a consistent up-and-down motion. Naturally, the teenager complains and resists, but eventually he does this same motion thousands of times until he becomes unconsciously competent, or masterful. After the boy completes this test and is ready to move into some real fighting techniques, the master surprises him again and hands him a piece of cloth, telling the boy to wax his car using a circular motion. Eventually, after the boy feels as though his arm is about to fall off from so much waxing, he realizes he can execute this motion without thinking. Eventually, the master begins to teach the boy to draw from these trained muscles and find relevance in the actual karate moves. The boy realizes this conditioning has not only made his muscles react automatically, but it has also demonstrated the discipline required for him to become great.

If you think about why people fail to fulfill their new year's resolutions or to implement their business initiatives, the answer usually boils down to the lack of discipline involved. Like the young student in *The Karate Kid*, people usually want to speed toward the finish line before undergoing the proper preparation. Understanding and adopting new themes is not easy. Try to find a connection between the business themes outlined here and your present business. Bring together some of your most committed team members and share these themes with them. Ask each one of them to pick a theme and try to articulate in his or her own words why it resonates on a personal level. Use analogies and metaphors that relate to your own personal experience to achieve a deeper understanding of the subject. Discuss the themes in the context of your business product, your people, and your processes. "Aggressive but realistic," for example, will mean something different for a dental practice than it will for a restaurant. Be specific. Identify instances when you have experienced the meaning of a theme—a time when you exceeded expectations, for instance, or when you listened particularly well to a client or to the market.

Trying to implement all of these themes at once is a little bit like eating an elephant in one bite. Still, the themes work together, and it is important not to ignore or downplay some at the expense of others. If you feel that some themes are less relevant to your situation than others, do not spend as much energy on them. However, do not ignore them, either. If you find these themes do not fully encompass all the conditions of your business (although I have not found any really missing elements), identify the missing puzzle piece and attempt to create and articulate a theme to fill the void. As in sports, you need to have the foundation down before you can move toward mastery and really see the fruits of these themes in your business.

Theme Mastery: Taking It to the Next Level

We are what we repeatedly do. Excellence, then, is not an act, but a habit.

—Aristotle

Becoming masterful at something develops magic. Through this mastery, you see the benefits and the returns of your time and energy. In becoming truly masterful, you and the members of your organization become unconsciously competent, and you begin to touch greatness. As you embrace these themes, they begin to take on an even greater importance once you start combining them. An almost unlimited number of combinations of these themes will enable you to discover the real answers to your business questions. As an example, think of a juggler. When he juggles three balls, it is not a big deal; in fact, it is sort of ordinary. When he adds a fourth and a fifth ball, you become impressed. Then, a really masterful juggler adds fire to the act, or juggles while riding a unicycle. At that point, you are on the edge of your seat, both being entertained and anxiously waiting to see if he will fail. Elevating the simple act of juggling to a more masterful level is what makes it come to life and become truly entertaining and memorable. While you continue developing the basics of understanding and improving your use of each theme individually, in the next chapter I will illustrate how the themes can be combined, like puzzle pieces, and fit together for your greater success. Many combinations make the themes useful, like tools, and you will need to choose the right tools for your particular situation. In the following chapter, I use a real situation in business growth to illustrate how, when these themes are combined, someone can achieve a higher level of success.

Assembling Themes

Life is the sum of all the choices.

—Albert Camus

As you begin to understand and embrace these themes, you will see their relevance to and dependence upon each other. Think of the themes as puzzle pieces. As you connect more and more pieces together, the image becomes clearer. Finally, you achieve the ultimate goal of combining all the pieces and creating the complete image. It may be preferable to find a corner piece with which to start, but doing so is not required. You can begin with any puzzle piece, or any business theme, to start the exercise. While it would be impossible to illustrate all the possible combinations or variations in this book, I will share a few examples of how they have connected together here.

"PEOPLE ARE YOUR GREATEST ASSET" + "1 + 1 = 3"

If you truly believe people are your greatest asset, you are always seeking creative ways to find better uses and achieve greater returns for this asset. Real synergistic thinking (the idea that the sum is greater than its parts) and results happen when you bring people together from different worlds to focus on a common goal or problem. Synergistic results often come from unexpected individuals working together. As I described earlier, when I explained the development of the bath division within our business, the quiet, unassuming project manager on our committee was the one who coined the theme of "production proven." This concept became a key filter for making decisions through the whole business-development design process. The entire direction of this division would have been dramatically different if we had not had this filter to guide us. By first seeing the people in the business as the greatest asset, then finding ways to leverage this asset through synergistic activities, our team conceived and developed real, successful solutions.

A key to combining themes like these two is believing in each separately; after that, you can see the benefit of combining them. You have to visually imagine the two themes combined. This is like seeing a baseball player and then visualizing him playing his position along with his team members on the field. Once you connect people and synergy, you will be able to look for opportunities to improve and grow your business. As in many aspects of our lives (sports, math, cooking, etc.), you need to have a good understanding of the individual parts to create a wonderful game, formula, or meal.

"PEOPLE ARE YOUR GREATEST ASSET" +
"1 + 1 = 3" +
"INVEST TIME TO IMPROVE"

Now, let's continue this example by adding a third theme to the formula. Suppose we begin with the belief that people are the greatest asset (they are the best vehicle for strong returns). Then we can use synergistic processes and thinking from these assets to develop new ideas. We need some conviction in the recipe to make it come to life. This conviction is the commitment we need to "invest time to improve." This theme shows commitment, and it also invokes the idea of keeping at something until you get it right. Investing time to improve gives you and your team members permission to do whatever it takes to get to the improvement level you are trying to achieve.

Let's return to my example of developing the bath division within our business. This took the right assembly of designers, production experts, marketing team members, and field personnel (all assets). It also took a synergistic process and creative discussions to get these unlikely people to brainstorm with each other. In addition, it took allocating the necessary time to improve and to get where we needed to get. We could not have achieved a positive result without the conviction to improve (that is, to build a better mousetrap). Many great ideas are never developed fully simply because people do not invest enough time in order to make them successful.

**"PEOPLE ARE YOUR GREATEST ASSET" +
"1 + 1 = 3" +
"INVEST TIME TO IMPROVE" +
"IT IS OUR OBLIGATION TO COMMUNICATE, NOT THE
RESPONSIBILITY OF OTHERS TO UNDERSTAND"**

In an effort to continue building upon this process of combining themes, let's add a fourth theme to the mix. Just as in preparing a meal, you need the right ingredients assembled in a skillful way, and you also need the right spices to bring the flavors to life. Going back to our example, you can assemble the great assets (people) along with a commitment to improve matters through a synergistic process, but you also need to communicate effectively during this process. Communication involves willingness to communicate, as well as how the communication is conveyed and who actually owns it. If team members commit to taking ownership of their own communication, they will make sure others understand key concepts and messages. This level of ownership may require creative methods of communication. Sometimes verbal communication alone is not always effective. The owner of the communication may chose diagrams, photos, or even metaphors as a more effective means of communicating.

During the development of the bath division at our company, the project manager referred to invoices for products specified in previous custom bathroom renovations that had created delays or required repairs. These invoices allowed him to illustrate which products to avoid on future projects since they were not "production proven." In addition, the designers used sketches to show visual illustrations of three bath renovation choices that should be presented within the program, adding further clarity for all. Then, the sales team used staged role plays to communicate how they would present the new bath program to clients. These role plays, as a method of communication, struck a chord with the marketing team members, who were responsible for the right language in the marketing pieces. The commitment to communication and communication ownership was the glue that held many other aspects of this process together. Without proper ownership, effective communication becomes very difficult.

"PEOPLE ARE YOUR GREATEST ASSET" +
"1 + 1 = 3" +
"INVEST TIME TO IMPROVE" +
"IT'S OUR OBLIGATION TO IMPROVE, NOT THE
RESPONSIBILITY OF OTHERS TO UNDERSTAND" +
"AGGRESSIVE BUT REALISTIC"

Let's take this assemblage process one step further and add a fifth theme. The theme of being aggressive but realistic establishes pace. Pace, or cadence, is very important to the growth of a business in terms of maintaining a healthy business culture and undertaking any project or initiative. It creates alignment within a team and gives you a check-up question to ask: "Is this solution/plan aggressive but realistic?" If you do not have a way to understand or align your team members in terms of pace and cadence, or you do not have a way to communicate this, the process can break down.

Once again let's use the bath division as an example. My team members and I needed the right importance placed on the people (assets), the synergistic process, a commitment of time to improve to accomplish our goal, and the right level of accountability and ownership related to proper communication. We also needed to properly pace ourselves both in developing the division and in determining what the new division would ultimately accomplish for the organization. If we had an individual or two who were moving along at an overly aggressive pace in the process, while others only inched things forward, it would have caused extreme frustration for all. If we had assumed, based on everyone's enthusiasm, that this division would have set new sales or profit records before it was properly tested, the likelihood of success would have been reduced. The theme of aggressive but realistic is both a measurement theme and a rallying cry for alignment. Unlike some themes that do not need mentioning because they become part of your day-to-day thinking and decision making, the theme of aggressive but realistic should relate to an active question asked and discussed by all.

As you can see, it is important to understand and embrace the individual themes, and they also become more powerful as you layer one on top of another. These combinations add richness and clarity to your business. They assist in your decision-making processes and overall business experiences.

My challenge to you is to first understand them as stand-alone themes; then, start to hook a couple together. At that point, you can really push the process and see the themes as a collection of puzzle pieces that, when put together, help you develop a vision and a culture that is positioned well for growth and success.

SUMMARY

We don't stop playing because we grow old;
we grow old because we stop playing.

—George Bernard Shaw

Often, a book summary is a period that ends a very long sentence. In other books, the summary is an exclamation point that unveils a secret or makes a profound statement. Occasionally, the book ending goes unnoticed and fades into the sunset. The summary of *Fit to Grow* is none of these.

This summary is a challenge. It encourages you to go back into the body of the book for the answers you need to grow. I have made enough bold statements and used plenty of metaphors to try to communicate my message. Now, I will stop writing, and you can start doing. In an effort to give you some guidance and direction, I would encourage you to begin by focusing on the right questions before jumping into the answers. The answers to these questions will give you both the motivation and the direction you need to be Fit to Grow.

QUESTIONS:
THE POWER OF QUESTIONS

When we have arrived at the question,
the answer is already near.

—Ralph Waldo Emerson

A wise friend once told me, "If you don't know the answer, at least know the question." In business and in life, asking the right questions and correctly framing those questions is critical in getting to the right solutions, answers, or directions. Today, more than ever, business has so many moving parts that it becomes more complicated, confusing, and overwhelming to come up with the right answers. Questions can simplify what appears very complex. Questions are tools that allow us to put a lens in focus. They better allow us to see what we have and where we should be heading in the future. Questions do not only test you; they also allow you to see how others in your business are aligned and where there are differences.

In reviewing the following questions, you again may want to go back and seek answers or find more clarity by revisiting an earlier chapter or theme. While I did not present the twelve themes as questions, I could have done so. You should spend some time reflecting on these questions. By writing down your responses for each and returning to these questions later, you will also see how dynamic your business is and how your answers change over time.

TEN IMPORTANT QUESTIONS

1. **What business am I in?**

   Nike's CEO once said, "We are not in the shoe business; we are in the marketing business."

   _____

   _____

   _____

2. **Why am I in business?**

   Three out of five businesses fail in the first five years. There are many ways to fulfill your professional passion. If your why is not sound enough, the risk of failure increases dramatically.

   _____

   _____

   _____

3. **What is my and the business's endgame?**

   Life is a journey, not a destination, but most journeys are heading somewhere. You do not need to know the specific answer, but it is important and asking the question helps you to stay on course.

   _____

   _____

   _____

4. How do I define success?

Is it money? Is it fame or power? Is it pride? Is it helping others? Defining success creates clarity and alignment for all.

_____

_____

_____

5. How fit is my business?

Once you understand business fitness, you should focus on your weaknesses, not just improving your strengths.

_____

_____

_____

6. How do I define growth?

Like success, growth can be defined in many ways. However, it must be defined companywide in order to have everyone pushing for the same goal.

_____

_____

_____

7. Am I positioned for growth?

Are you focused and committed? Do you have the capital or resources for growth?

_____

_____

_____

8. **Are others aligned with my vision and goals?**

   When was the last time you asked?

   _____

   _____

   _____

9. **Do my team members and I have a plan?**

   A plan can be notes on the back of a napkin or it can be
   an elaborate blueprint.

   _____

   _____

   _____

10. **Are you Fit to Grow?**

   _____

   _____

   _____

Turn this page for a preview of Mark Richardson's book "How Fit Is Your Business?"

Foreword

Although both "business" and "fitness" appear in the title of this book, it has little to do with helping you achieve good physical fitness, nor will it teach you anything about how to start up a health club. The business the title refers to is the one you're already running, and the fitness it promises is not physical health, but the health of your business.

The first time I heard Mark Richardson apply the metaphor of health and fitness to business concepts was five years ago during a presentation he gave at a one-day conference for remodeling contractors. It began, as so many of Mark's presentations do, with a series of questions for the audience.

"If I asked you to name three things that are clear markers of good physical health and well-being, what would they be?" Mark asked.

"Low cholesterol," someone quickly answered. "Normal blood pressure," someone else added; then "proper weight" from the back of the room.

Obviously pleased with both the answers and how fast the audience responded, Mark kept the momentum going with a question about the tools doctors might use to measure physical health. He quickly got more good answers: thermometer, scale, blood test, treadmill.

"What would we do if our cholesterol were too high?"

"Stop eating fatty foods."

"What about being overweight, what then?"

"Go on a diet."

"How about high blood pressure?"

"See a doctor for a prescription."

More questions; more good, quick answers. Mark had made his point: we all have a clear idea of what it means to be physically healthy, and we all know what to do to get well again if we're not in such good shape. Now he went to the heart of the matter.

"Let's think about your business," Mark began. "What three things are clear markers of good business health."

Silence. Then a barely audible "Good sales" from the back of the room. More silence. Mark looked around, and repeated the question. Someone took a guess: "Profit?" Then someone else added, "Good referrals?"

It was clear to everyone that the answers to this new question hadn't come as quickly or with the confidence of the answers about physical health. Mark had the audience right where he wanted them.

"Sales, profit, referrals—good," he repeated. "And what tools do we use to measure them?

Silence again. "Money in the bank," someone finally offered, stirring some nervous laughter. "Lots of work lined up," someone else added.

"And if our business is unhealthy, what do we do to get back on track?" Silence.

What happened in that room over the next hour was the abridged version of what you're about to read. Mark led the audience through a ten-point business fitness "checkup," asking attendees to rate themselves and their companies on each component, then explaining what the results could tell them about the health of the business. Mark's objective was to transfer the notion of physical health and fitness, something everyone in the audience knew and understood, to the way we think about business. It was a clever idea that clicked with the audience. As one of the speakers on the program, I had the opportunity to hear it many more times over the next few weeks, and it clicked with every audience.

After the speaking tour ended, I didn't think much about the business fitness checkup again until Mark mentioned it two years later over lunch at Café Deluxe in Bethesda, Md. I had been editing Mark's column for Remodeling magazine for a number of years, and we made a habit of getting together for lunch every couple of months. Through the exchange of ideas in the column and those meetings, we had come to recognize how much alike our thinking was when it came to issues affecting small businesses. In one way, this made sense because we both had connections to the remodeling business; in my case, I had been a remodeler and custom home builder for 20 years before I started editing magazines for contractors; and Mark had worked as an architectural designer before turning to business management of a remodeling firm. What was a bit surprising, however, was that we saw eye to eye on so many issues despite the fact that Mark's business was literally 100 times bigger than mine had ever been. It seemed clear to both of us that some things were true of all businesses no matter how big or small, and irrespective of the product or service that they delivered.

Soon, "the book" was on the agenda every time we met. Deciding whether or not to proceed was never a question of the topic or its timeliness, it was more a matter of figuring out how to fit it into our schedules. I'm glad we found the time because, even with all of the business books on the market, I think there are several unique things about this one.

First, a fitness checkup and prescription for business health is not merely a clever idea, it works. This isn't just my opinion. I have seen the looks on the faces of Mark's audiences when he leads the live version of this check-up. And I have talked with people who have attended Mark's presentations and used the checkup to identify and correct weaknesses in their businesses.

Second, whereas the live 60-minute version I first witnessed addressed mainly the fitness check-up, the book by virtue of its length also provides a prescription for improvement in each of the critical areas. The simple rating system is a remarkably accurate tool for diagnosing "illness" within a business, and the corresponding improvement sections of the book provide step-by-step "treatments" on how to nurse it back to health. It doesn't promise overnight miracles; in fact, the approach is deliberate and incremental. Businesses don't grow ill over night and there are no shortcuts to making them healthy again.

Finally, the process of diagnosis and prescription put forth in these pages is repeatable. It is designed to be revisited again and again as a business changes in response to internal or external forces. In fact, a central theme of this book is the importance of constantly monitoring a business's "vital signs." Business is complex, and success is a moving target. Efforts to improve in one area draw resources away from other parts of the business, and even incremental changes can have far-reaching effects.

Although Mark's business experience comes mainly from the remodeling industry, I believe the principles put forth here apply to small businesses of virtually any type. The health and fitness metaphor does the heavy lifting with regard to the overall idea of diagnosing fitness and prescribing treatment to restore health, but the main thing is the process it is used to describe. I have no doubt that anyone who makes a genuine effort to follow the step-by-step checkup and apply the suggestions for improvement will gain new insight into what makes them successful and what is holding them back from even greater success.

Sal Alfano

Introduction

"When you look at the sun, you see no shadows "
-Helen Keller

Many years ago, while flipping through TV channels, I came across an infomercial on personal weight loss. I feel the same way about paid programming on TV as most other people—may the buyer beware!—but this program interested me for two reasons. First, the program promised a weight loss of ten pounds in twenty-one days, which struck a chord with me, because I had about fifty pounds to lose. Second, the program was designed around a methodical, easy to comprehend process, beginning with small but well-defined baby steps, and then increasing in intensity day after day. This incremental system appealed to me, so I ordered the program and began the process. The results were liberating. Not only did I lose the fifty pounds over a period of few months, I went on to participate in one-hundred-mile cycling marathons called "century rides," something I would never have considered possible. More important, I learned a technique for improvement and change that I was able to apply to other areas of my personal and business life.

My first attempt to translate this process into another part of my world was to develop and author an audio program called The 30-Day Remodeling Business Fitness Program. I guided the listener through a methodical, step-by-step process that began with taking inventory of the business, then developing plans for improvement, and finally rolling out and monitoring the changes. While this "fitness" program was well received and continues to be relevant, it was missing a key element: it didn't answer the question, "What is a fit business?" It is difficult to understand and improve on anything if you don't have a benchmark against which to measure progress. This benchmark not only allows you to look at your own history but also gives a means to compare to other businesses.

Since I had already started using the metaphor of fitness, it seemed only natural to draw the parallel between personal health and fitness, and business fitness. By connecting the dots between personal and business fitness, we remove some of the mystery from the process of improvement. We can take an aspect of our lives that we all live and breathe with every day and use it to find new but less obvious relationships and meaning in our businesses. Imagine how difficult it would be to develop a plan for weight loss and personal fitness if you did not have a clear image of what fitness meant or even some basic tools, like a scale, to measure it.

In this book, I begin by discussing why we have such a clear image of what personal fitness is but such a fuzzy picture of what business fitness is. This leads me to a breakdown of some business misconceptions that often lead us off on the wrong track. Next, I will bring you and your business into the examining room and conduct a ten-point business fitness checkup with a scoring system that will give you a foundation for a proper prescription. I will then show you how to interpret these results to establish a benchmark as a tool to measure your business and to compare it to other businesses. The ten criteria in the checkup also create a forum for determining specific areas where your business needs improvement. Finally, like any good doctor, I will set the stage for you to come back and have an annual checkup to monitor your progress.

Throughout this book, I use examples from everyday life to remove the confusion and mystery of business health and fitness. Business can be very complicated, but by breaking it down into small parts and creating a system for evaluation and improvement, I believe I can make business fitness easier to comprehend. As with our personal health and fitness, we need to have a clear image of what business health is before we can ever attempt to achieve it.

Misconceptions of Business Fitness

"Whoever said, 'It's not whether you win or
lose that counts,' probably lost."
- Martina Navratilova

Whether it is in our personal lives or our businesses, an incorrect belief, thinking something is good when it is not, can really throw us off course. For example, it used to be a widely held belief that fitness was simply a matter of training as hard as you could for as long as you could. "No pain, no gain" was the rallying cry, and everyone from weekend enthusiasts to professional athletes focused on training regimens that constantly ratcheted up the pressure. Today, athletes and trainers have learned that working harder is not the best way to make progress. They know that our bodies need a recovery period, and that alternating strenuous workouts with more relaxed routines sets the foundation for better results.

In the same way, there are many common misconceptions about what makes for a successful business. Erroneous beliefs about business health and fitness affect our day-to-day decisions and give us a false sense of confidence. Some of these misconceptions are small and some are large, but they all send the wrong signal and, if followed, will drive us off course. Imagine if your bathroom scale was slightly miscalibrated, and it appeared that you had lost an extra two or three pounds when in fact you had gained five. Or what if a blood test revealed a false positive for a serious disorder? Though different in severity, both of these examples would have a strong effect on your emotions, your self-image, and your decisions about what to do next.

Every industry or business category has its own pet beliefs about what constitutes a sign of good business health. Here are some that I encounter most often in the remodeling industry.

"We are booked out for six months." Over the years, I have found it interesting that many small- to medium-sized remodeling businesses gauge how well they are doing based on their backlog of work. Often when I am addressing a group of business owners and someone says he is booked out for six months or more, I ask him how it makes him feel. I have asked this question hundreds of times to a variety of audiences, and the answers I generally get are "Great," "Confident," or "Secure." But I get a very different answer when I ask the same audience to consider how a manufacturer in the same position would feel. Imagine for a moment the effect on the business of a manufacturer of windows or faucets who couldn't deliver a product to a new client for six months. It would be disastrous; the long wait for delivery would drive away even their most loyal customers.

If you believe that the longer you are booked out the better, then you are being fooled by a misconception. You may believe that things are good when, in fact, you may be losing market share. Yes, everyone ought to have a backlog—but it needs to be the right size, one that allows your processes and systems to function properly. Too little backlog and you may find yourself scrambling for your next piece of business; too great a backlog and your customer base may disappear or change its character. Understanding what makes for the right amount of backlog is part of the process that leads to a fit business. Finding the balance and using *that* as a target is where healthy businesses want to be.

"Almost all my business comes from personal referrals." As you think about your business, how does this statement make you feel? For most of my audiences, the response is very positive. "It makes me feel proud," I hear people say, or, "This is a great way to position ourselves." While I would agree that every business benefits from personal referrals, there may be another way to think about this. When all of your business comes from personal referrals, you are not really in control of your future. If the economy slows down or a specific market changes, you need to be able to generate new clients. Over-reliance on referrals can make your marketing "muscles" weak; when you need some "heavy lifting," your strength will not be able to handle it. Most businesses with a very high percentage of revenue from personal referrals ride a rollercoaster from good times to bad. Their growth is not as sustainable as it should be, and they see only modest gains over long periods of time. Can you get the phone to ring with out depending on your existing client base?

"Our sales are up by 30 percent over last year." Imagine you are at a reception and share this news with an old friend. You're probably feeling pretty good about yourself and your team. But if I were to look behind the curtain, I doubt you would get a slap on the back from me. More businesses have imploded because of an excessively high rate of growth in sales than the reverse. Too much change too fast is unhealthy. We all know the dangers of crash diets when it comes to our personal health. Unless you are severely obese, very few health professionals would encourage you to lose five or ten pounds in a week.

Our bodies are like machines, and so are our businesses. A machine is designed to run at an optimum speed for ideal performance. If you exceed that limit, it may affect efficiency and, ultimately, life expectancy. In business, systems and processes are designed for a specific volume of sales; checks and balances are in place to help maintain proper quality of product and service. These limits should not be exceeded by too wide a margin. The levels of investment and infrastructure should be in sync with both short- and long-term goals. Unless the business is a start-up, huge growth in sales is not generally a positive sign for health and fitness.

"We just landed the largest contract ever!" Generally, a remodeling contractor makes a statement like this with a lot of enthusiasm. Everyone dreams of "landing the big one," and when it happens, most assume that their days of struggling to get their business going are over. Occasionally, however, I get a chance to follow up with these business owners six or twelve months later, and I always make it a point to ask them how they are feeling about that home run deal. With few exceptions, the enthusiasm has been replaced with regret that they ever landed that big fish.

Often when I speak to remodeling contractors, I ask the audience about the ideal project size for their companies. Usually, the answers range from "It doesn't matter" to "The bigger the better."

Sometimes, though, someone will shout out a specific number, like $72,500. The audience usually reacts with nervous laughter, but then it begins to sink in. Whereas most remodelers believe that if they are competent to do small projects then they should be equally equipped to do large projects, and vice versa, I believe that there is a sweet spot in business—and, more importantly, that knowledge of what that sweet spot is should guide business decisions.

If you believe "bigger is better" or "size doesn't matter," then you may be misguided. Distractions or false hopes in business can lead to more problems than solutions.

"We are very busy." Even though most business owners today do not equate being busy with success, it would be remiss not to highlight this misconception because people in certain roles are particularly susceptible to it. It may be, for example, that a change in market conditions or the overall selling environment is keeping salespeople busier than ever chasing down new clients or spending more time than ever as "unpaid consultants" or "professional researchers" for prospective customers. Although they feel like they are making progress, when you analyze a typical day in their lives, you realize that they are spending more hours getting less accomplished. This same dynamic commonly occurs in people with management and client support responsibilities. They may be moving at a frenetic pace, spending more time than usual "putting out fires," but all of this activity contributes nothing to the company's success and often works against it.

Activity is often mistaken as a sign of good business health. When we feel busy, it's easy to assume that we are moving the enterprise forward. After all, no one wants to be the Maytag man. We all want to believe that what we are doing is important and meaningful. Being busy does that, but it is not necessarily a positive sign of health.

Every business owner can, with a little reflection, come up with more examples like these. Why is it that so many of the commonsense observations we make about our business health and fitness are so far from the mark? More importantly, what observations should we be making to get a true picture of where our businesses are strong and where they need improvement?

Introduction to the Checkup

"The future ain't what it used to be"
- Yogi Berra

A s we have discussed in previous chapters, personal health and fitness is something we can easily recognize. We also have little difficulty naming specific ways we can measure our physical health. We all understand that we can see some signs of health with the naked eye but that others require complex testing. All of these pieces fit together to form our image of what it means to be healthy. Consciously or not, we constantly monitor our health, and in most cases we can easily tell when our level of fitness has dropped.

I have chosen deliberately to present a business fitness test in the familiar form of a personal physical checkup. The more closely you can follow that parallel process, the more you will gain from this exercise. You know, for example, that the results of a physical exam will not be as helpful if you skip any of the steps. The same is true of this business checkup. It is a process and a system that should be followed step by step. I will offer plenty of guidance along the way, but you are your own proctor. The more honest you are with your answers, the more useful the results of the checkup will be.

In the checkup itself, each business fitness element is weighted equally, and you will be asked to rate each one. The scoring system is simple: the scale ranges from 1 on the low side to 10 as the maximum. Fractional scores are okay, too; recording a 7.5 after some serious reflection is better than rounding up to 8 or down to 7 just for the sake of using round numbers.

When you reach the end of the checkup, you will have recorded ten scores, one for each of the ten fitness criteria. Although the scores are subjective, I have found that they produce consistent results. A score of 10 indicates that your business is performing at its peak. Use a score of 10 if you feel you are far above your competition in the relevant area and there is little or no room for improvement.

A score of 5 indicates average performance—like earning a grade of "C" in school. An element scored with a 5 may not be causing you much pain at the moment, but it represents an opportunity for improvement. Moving from a score of 5 to a score of 6 or 7 would clearly create a more positive picture.

A score of 1 means that this aspect of your business is critically ill and improving performance should move to the top of your to-do list. The good news is that efforts to improve a score of 1 often show quick results because there is nowhere to go but up. It's much easier to move a score of 1 to a score of 2 or 3 than it is to move an 8 to a 9.

Each chapter explains the fitness criteria in terms you can easily recognize in your particular business. You still need to read carefully, however, because my experience is that much of what you will read is new information. Or at least it represents a new way of thinking about your business. On the other hand, while unfamiliar material may appeal to you most, it would be a mistake to ignore sections in which the subject matter seems too basic. It is in just these areas that you are more likely to uncover false assumptions or discover new ways of thinking about familiar issues. Remember, too, that although each chapter is designed to be read independently and scored separately, they are like the pieces of a jigsaw puzzle; there is real benefit in looking at each piece in relation to all of the others.

There are no "right" answers in this fitness checkup, and researching and gathering data will not help your results. Adopting a balanced frame of mind, however, will make a difference. It is human nature to look into the mirror and exaggerate what you see, for better or worse. So if you are going through a personal or professional crisis, either check those issues at the door before diving into this checkup or postpone the checkup until some of the turmoil has been resolved. If you have many distractions that could make it difficult to focus, try to isolate yourself from e-mail or cell phone access for a couple of hours to concentrate on the task at hand.

Pace and timing are also important to the outcome of this checkup. Some may find it beneficial to read through all of the checkup sections, and then go back to each one to record a score. Others may prefer to score themselves the first time through. No single approach works better than any other, so try to find what works for you. Remember, too, that you can return again and again to repeat the checkup. In fact, it is my hope that the results will be so useful and you will see such improvement that you will make it a regular practice to take the test and analyze your score, just like an annual physical.

This checkup is a personal process, and you may want your scores to remain private. I do recommend, however, that after you have taken this test, you give a fitness book to some of your key team members or to your spouse. They will have insights about your business that only their unique perspective can generate. Plus, their direct participation in the checkup will make it easier to implement any improvements that the test reveals are needed. Again, you will get more valuable information if you let the book speak for itself and avoid guiding or influencing team members' scoring.

With all of this talk of scores and results, it is easy to lose sight of the fact that the whole purpose is to have a meaningful experience, one that is both a journey and a destination. Although the goal is to end up with an overall score for your business fitness, the process of thinking about the criteria and evaluating how your company measures up is equally valuable, if not more important. Regardless of how you score yourself, the checkup itself should get the wheels turning on ways you can improve.

Finally, while it is important to avoid being too casual in your approach to this checkup, you should also guard against becoming too obsessed. Make this checkup meaningful, and make it a positive tool for your business, but also make it fun. Business is a game—a difficult one, but a game nonetheless. You will play the game better if you are having fun.

Part Two:

The Business
Fitness
Checkup

Knowing Your Numbers

"If it doesn't matter who wins or loses, then why do we keep score?"
-Vince Lombardi

When it comes to personal health and fitness, we can measure vital statistics in a variety of ways. Some, such as weight or basic stamina, are pretty obvious from causal observation. Others, such as blood pressure and cholesterol levels require simple testing by your doctor to determine whether or not you are within healthy ranges. More complicated, targeted testing may be required if you or your doctor has a particular concern or if you have reached a certain age.

Measurements like these are useful to anyone concerned about remaining reasonably healthy. But to a person committed to moving beyond average health and achieving a higher level of fitness, these kinds of metrics are even more compelling. A person committed to fitness will focus on these vital statistics not only to establish a baseline and monitor progress, but also to create a plan for diet and exercise.

Like your personal health, your business also has vital statistics. And as is true of health metrics, some aspects of your business are easier to measure than others. Early in your journey to better business fitness, pay attention to the obvious numbers first. Then, as you improve, you can begin to use more complicated diagnostic tools to measure other critical business functions.

As you reflect on the various ways that numbers relate to business fitness, you might notice that one obvious success measurement is missing—profitability. I'll treat this critical element in a separate chapter later on, so be patient and stick to the checkup process.

Vital numbers. All businesses have certain numbers that are essential to monitor. Retailers know, for example, that the average spend per customer is an important benchmark to watch, while in food services, managers keep an eye on the number of seatings during a specific time period. In the remodeling business, the most important numbers to monitor are total sales, gross profit margin (percentage and dollars), overhead expense, and percentage of completion. More sophisticated remodeling companies will also watch the number of inquiries or leads, the cost per lead, sales close rates, and average project size.

If numbers like these are checked frequently enough, even slight fluctuations can impart valuable intelligence about how a business is performing. More importantly, these measurements serve as an early warning system that gives managers and owners enough time to make adjustments.

Knowing what to monitor is only half the battle. The real work comes with creating and managing the systems that deliver the critical statistics at regular intervals. Owners of small businesses should be able to keep the most vital numbers in their heads, but all business owners should have their company's vital numbers at their fingertips.

How do you measure up? Do you know which parts of your business you should be monitoring? Do you have ways to gather critical statistics weekly, monthly, quarterly, or annually as required? Can you recite your company's vital numbers without having to look them up? If you had to look them up, would you know where to find them or would you have to ask the bookkeeper?

Guided by numbers. Knowing your company's critical numbers is only the first step; more important is what you do with this knowledge. If you are on a diet, knowing that you gained two pounds after a holiday feast is only useful if it prompts you to push away from the table the next day; it helps you reach your weight loss goal only if it spurs you to increase your exercise for a couple of days and have the discipline to check your weight again a week later.

In the same way, knowing your numbers is only useful if it leads to change and re-measurement. In my studies of business behavior, I find that the difference between knowing and acting on what you know is often what separates average businesses from great ones. In today's business environment, it's easy to become overwhelmed with the number of balls you have to keep in the air. That makes it difficult to make room for review of key metrics in your daily routine. Most business owners focus attention on the business's vital signs only when symptoms of illness are impossible to ignore, but by then it is very tough to get on the road to recovery. Owners of healthy businesses have mastered the discipline of including vital statistics into their day-to-day decision-making process.

Knowing your numbers also keeps you grounded in reality. Our emotional ups and downs play games with our perceptions and can affect our ability to evaluate accurately how we are performing. We may exaggerate a small failure into an attitude of defeat that holds us back from reaching our goals. Or our exhilaration over our success may lead us into arrogance or complacency. Understanding key metrics enables business owners to set goals they know they can achieve without too much risk.

Do you communicate critical business metrics to all members of your organization? Are critical statistics discussed regularly at staff meetings? Do team members at all levels rely on metrics as a basis for action?

Regular review. If you're trying to lose weight, you might climb onto a scale more often than someone whose weight is at an optimal level. But some frequency intervals make more sense than others. Weighing yourself every hour would be foolish because the variance from one measurement to the next would be so small. Monitoring your weight daily might be okay if you were seriously overweight because a daily weigh-in would show some progress. Otherwise, however, too short an interval might send false signals about how well your diet or exercise regimen is working. Weekly monitoring is probably ideal in the early stages, increasing to monthly as you come closer to your weight goal. These frequency intervals would give you measurable results that allow for simple adjustments to help you stay on track without overreacting.

What's good for a weight loss program is also good for your business. Reviewing your numbers regularly is essential if you want to take your business to a higher level. It is not a matter of being more intelligent than other business owners, it is about having the discipline to work smart. Most successful business leaders put a priority on making these kinds of activities into success habits. A "success habit" is an activity or way of thinking that not only contributes to a positive outcome but also does so because, through repetition and practice, it has become second nature. For example, most good pilots have trained themselves to check altitude, air speed, weather patterns, fuel levels, and other gauges on their instrument panel every few minutes without having to think deliberately about it.

New Year's resolutions work—or fail to work—for the same reason. Most people who make New Year's resolutions in January fall off the wagon by February or March. Rarely does this happen because the resolutions were unrealistic or stupid, or because the behavior of others interfered. Resolutions are broken because most people don't monitor their progress, so the resolution never becomes a success habit. By the time they realize they have drifted off course, the pain of getting back on target is too great, so they quit trying.

What is the right monitoring cycle for key business indicators? It depends, not only on your product or service, but also on your present business health. For example, if you are in a service business that bills clients at an hourly rate, you might want to take the pulse on billings once a day, or at least once a week. If, on the other hand, your business involves larger contracts, such as real estate transactions or construction projects, the appropriate monitoring cycle may be monthly or even quarterly.

The important question for this business fitness element is this: do you have a review cycle for your important business metrics and does that review actually take place?

Financial tools. If you didn't know how to use a scale, it would be tough to monitor your weight. If you weren't able to make any sense out of the information on the food labels at the grocery store, then it would be difficult to make good buying decisions to prepare balanced meals.

Your business has some standard financial tools, too. These tools not only help you to understand the health and fitness of your business, they also allow an objective observer from outside your business to guide and advise you.

The most basic financial tools are your profit and loss statement and your balance sheet. Understanding these reports doesn't mean you have to know how to prepare them; it just means you are conversant enough with them to make sound judgments based on the information they hold. I don't understand how a nutritionist determines the percentage of fat in certain foods, but I do understand how to read food labels. I know how much fat is too much, and based on that I can make a judgment about which foods to consume. Similarly, I don't need to know how a digital scale works to understand the numbers in the display.

Do you understand the basic financial tools that help you determine your business health?

Budget. Imagine for a moment a pilot who did not track the progress of a flight to make sure he was following the flight plan he filed before takeoff. Would the plane full of passengers reach the correct destination? And if it did, would it arrive on time?

A budget is a businesses flight plan. It provides the means for you to determine what your projected revenue will be for the year, and to estimate what you think you will need to spend to hit that target. A budget also shows how much profit you expect to put in your pocket or invest further into the business. Without a budget, you have no flight plan—a very risky proposition for even the most experienced pilots. And like other vital statistics, you should review your budget at least monthly; otherwise, your business may fly off course.

It doesn't matter whether a budget is simple or complex, so long as it includes all of the critical variables. Some businesses may need just ten or twenty line items in their budget; others may need hundreds. Nor does it matter who prepares the budget. Some business leaders do the prep work themselves, others rely on an accountant or financial advisor to handle the budget, leaving them free to focus on other aspects of the business.

There is no debate, however, about the fact that there needs to be a budget, and someone needs to track it regularly. How does your company score when it comes to budget?

History. Any business more than a few years old has a set of historical numbers that describe its performance over time. This is an important record for a number of reasons. For one thing, it keeps you from repeating your mistakes, and it makes it easier for you to duplicate your successes. A business history also gives you perspective and helps you to recognize the cadence and pace of your company.

To help understand what I mean by cadence and pace, imagine a veteran competitive runner preparing for a ten-kilometer race. She relies on the experience of past races for everything from pre-race workouts and diet to actual race tactics. The history of performance in previous races helps her determine what pace she can sustain and how much water to drink to maximize efficiency. Without this history, she will almost certainly not perform as well and may even be injured.

Your business history works in the same way. It helps you to know when to invest marketing dollars to realize the best returns, to understand optimal staff levels and hours of operation, and to determine how much growth your company can comfortably sustain.

History should not be followed blindly, however. Circumstances change, and what worked in the past may not work as well in the future. But a healthy business cannot ignore its history.

History is as real as it gets. It's not debatable, it's not subjective, and it doesn't care how you are feeling today. As businesses move to higher levels of fitness and health, they use historical data to drill into trends and complex ratios that are less obvious.

Score This Fitness Key

While all of these elements are interrelated, it is possible to perform better in some than in others. Review each element of this fitness key:

Vital numbers: Do you know your company's vital statistics?

Guided by numbers: Do you rely on vital statistics as a basis for action?

Regular review: How often do you review important business metrics?

Financial tools: Can you interpret a profit and loss statement and a balance sheet?

Budget: Does your company operate with a budget? Does someone monitor the budget regularly?

History: Do you use past performance to guide future plans?

Do you know your numbers? Rate your organization on a scale of 1 to 10. (Use decimals if needed.)

Knowing Your Numbers. Write in your score:

_____

Want to read more about business fitness and take the complete checkup?

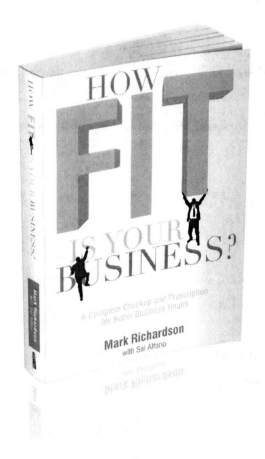

To order a copy go to Amazon.com
Title: How Fit Is Your Business
ISBN# 978-1601940193

For Bulk orders please contact Mark at:
mrichardson@mgrichardson.com or 301.275.0208

ABOUT THE AUTHOR

MARK G. RICHARDSON's involvement in construction, design and business spans more than three decades. A graduate of the School of Architecture at Virginia Tech, his career has been defined by leadership and an entrepreneurial spirit. As the former Co-Chairman and President of Case, he led the growth of over 1,000% by expanding services and market reach. For ten years he hosted "At Home with Mark Richardson," a weekly radio show dedicated to bringing a slice of the remodeling industry to consumers and practitioners alike. Mark's passion for teaching and speaking generally takes complex ideas and simplifies things for diverse groups.

Mark is a guest lecturer for MBA programs at Virginia Tech, Georgetown University, Maryland University and George Washington University. He serves as a business advisor to many business sectors from small practices to major corporations. In 2007 he developed a series of online business workshops and videos designed to offer professional, effective and intelligent business practices from business fitness to sales and marketing strategies.

Mark is a Fellow at Harvard University's Joint Center for Housing Studies and sits on many boards including GE Capital, Roxul, Better Business Bureau, Revere Bank and Advantage Media Group. He is also a regular columnist for *Professional Remodeler, Professional Builder, Big Growers* and *Residential Lighting* magazines. Other Mark Richardson vehicles include: The Remodeling Thirty Day Fitness Program, Remodeling Live, Prime, The Pro Expo and Business over Breakfast series. In 2008 Mark was inducted into the National Association of Home Builders Hall of Fame.

Mark continues to write, speak and consult with diverse organizations in an effort to help them improve and grow. He can be reached at mrichardson@mgrichardson.com.

CPSIA information can be obtained
at www.ICGtesting.com
Printed in the USA
FFOW02n1440180814
6917FF